A MAN TO HEAL DIFFERENCES:
Essays and Talks on St. Francis de Sales

Elisabeth Stopp
(1911-1996)

A MAN TO HEAL DIFFERENCES:
Essays and Talks on St. Francis de Sales

By
Elisabeth Stopp

SAINT JOSEPH'S UNIVERSITY PRESS

PHILADELPHIA

LIBRARY OF CONGRESS CATALOG CARD NUMBER 96-068191

ISBN 0-916101-22-3 PAPER

PUBLISHED BY:

SAINT JOSEPH'S UNIVERSITY PRESS
5600 CITY LINE AVENUE
PHILADELPHIA, PENNSYLVANIA 19131-1395

SAINT JOSEPH'S UNIVERSITY PRESS IS A MEMBER
OF THE ASSOCIATION OF JESUIT UNIVERSITY PRESSES

COVER: ST. FRANCIS DE SALES IN 1622. THE THURNFELD PORTRAIT
(MONASTERY OF THE VISITATION, BAD HALL, AUSTRIA)

TABLE OF CONTENTS

FOREWORD

It is an honour to have been invited to write a foreword to this collection of writings by Dr. Elisabeth Stopp, a friend of many years standing. I received much from her and her late husband Dr. Frederick J. Stopp, during the years when I was at Cambridge University, as an undergraduate from 1947 to 1950, then as Chaplain to Catholic students from 1977 to 1982. Both were Germanists, both University Lecturers, Freddy later becoming a Reader, in the Faculty of Modern and Medieval Languages. Both contributed a great deal to the life of the Catholic Chaplaincy at Fisher House. Freddy, as he was always called, was a Fellow of Gonville and Caius College; Elisabeth was a Fellow of Girton College. Since they had no children they brought to the academic community not only their intellectual gifts, but also an affective quality which found expression in the hospitality of their home in Drosier Road, extended to their many friends at home and especially abroad.

Theirs was a unique partnership, and it is exemplified by an anecdote which has become part of Cambridge folklore. The story goes that, at the beginning of each academic year, Elisabeth would preface her lecture by announcing her name and subject, adding: "If you have come here under the impression that I am Dr. F. J. Stopp and am about to lecture on sixteenth-century German literature, you should go to lecture room such-and-such where my husband is waiting to address you." Whereupon half the class would get up and leave, to encounter on the stairs an approaching group of undergraduates who had received the corresponding declaration from Freddy and were eager to start their course in German Romantic poets and authors with his wife.

Elisabeth had been educated entirely in England, but her Austrian family background and connections with France gave her ready access to European culture. She was equally fluent in

French and German. As such, she was adept at seeking "the precise connotation and emotional resonance of words"; she was a craftsman in words, a quality which she was happy to recognize in St. Francis de Sales ("*Meditations on the Church* [1595-96]," 52). The right use of language was for her of supreme importance, and she notes with approval the conviction of St. Francis' first biographer that "[i]t is . . . something like a religious duty to use words well and for an upright purpose" ("The First Biography [1624]," 152). With this went her ability, as a careful historian, for evoking a period and for describing its intellectual climate. Her success in investigating the connection between writers and assessing the literary influences which had an effect on them makes the pages which follow a delight.

Her careful scholarship, her passion for *le mot juste* was carried into her daily life and conversation without a trace of pedantry. Her conversation was lively, well-informed and amusing, sustained by her high voice with its attractively mocking tone. She was very much a Cambridge personality with that typical combination of formality and informality. One remembers Elisabeth cycling along the streets and lanes of the university town, with her academic gown rolled up in the pannier on the handlebars with her shopping.

Beneath the literary sensibility, Elisabeth lived out the spirituality of Christian humanism, a spirituality which is no stranger to the cross. Elisabeth nursed her husband through a long illness and felt his absence daily after his death in 1979. She wrote well of the saints because she shared their quest for God and their eagerness to serve Him. This did not exclude self-doubt and self-reproach. Fr. Allan White, O.P., who preached the homily at her Requiem Mass on 14 November 1996, said: ". . . the Christian is no stranger to the desert. Elisabeth was familiar especially in her latter years with its spiritual landscape . . . Those who go out into the desert abandon the illusion of self-sufficiency to live in total obedience to God." On her lonely journey, Elisabeth had two unseen companions, St. Francis de Sales and St. Jeanne Françoise de Chantal. May this book lead others to experience the help of their guiding hand!

✠ M. N. L. Couve de Murville
Archbishop of Birmingham (U.K.)

PREFACE

Gathered here for the first time, these essays and lectures of Elisabeth Stopp draw a marvelous and lifelike portrait of Francis de Sales, the seventeenth-century bishop, writer and saint. What emerges is a personal portrait reflecting Dr. Stopp's lifelong interest in and study of Francis, his friends and his times. As a onetime Lecturer in the Faculty of Modern and Medieval Languages at the University of Cambridge, she specialized in the German Romantics, but she was drawn early on to write about Francis de Sales and his friend, Jane de Chantal. Even though the original publication dates of these pieces ranges over four decades, the portrait they present is gradually and consistently filled out. Certain characteristics of this portrayal stand out.

Frequently Dr. Stopp stresses Francis' roots in Savoy, where he was born and where—apart from a few sojourns elsewhere—he served as priest and bishop. While his education and culture were French and Italian, and his Church ties European, he never lost touch with his own people and the land. While he would impress many prominent people in the great cities he visited, he preferred the smaller dimensions, the slower pace and the ordinary people of Annecy and its environs.

Second, as Dr. Stopp portrays him, Francis had profound affinities with the medieval world as well as with the modern. He lived in a time of cultural and religious upheaval and transition, and "without being traditionalist in a negative way, he was not 'modern' either in his own time" ("Medieval Affinities: St. Francis of Assisi," 163). He was steeped in the Catholic tradition: the biblical books he knew almost by heart, the Church Fathers and the medieval scholars and saints, especially his patrons, Francis and Bonaventure, without overlooking Thomas, Bernard and many others. At the same time twentieth-century readers will find him quite modern because of the emerging vernacular language he used and influenced; because of his insight into human interiority which made him a gifted "psychologist" before the term; because of his teaching, which, as Pope Paul VI was to say, anticipated the Second Vatican Council in several specific ways.

Elisabeth Stopp also and especially portrays Francis as a writer. She attributes the uniqueness and lasting attractiveness of his writings not so much to what he said, but to how he said it— to his literary style. For example, the *Introduction to a Devout Life* was one of many similar spiritual guides written for lay people in his time, but his is the only one with "high literary value" and thus has lasted and become a classic ("The Art of the Writer," 77).

Of course, Francis never set out to be a writer; he set out to be in the service of the Church. As part of his study of the humanities at Clermont College in Paris, he learned the art of letter writing, and later as part of his ministry he wrote letters— many of them marvelous letters of spiritual direction. In time, again for pastoral reasons, he was led to write books, and to see them through to publication, and in the case of the *Introduction*, to a further, much expanded edition.

Dr. Stopp sees Francis as having not only style, but also uncommon substance, "an essentially personal synthesis" ("The Art of the Writer," 77), namely, the divine call of all Christians to holiness (devotion), and the concrete means of growing toward it in any life setting. This synthesis is present, almost from the outset, though it was expressed differently in different works according to the purpose and scope of each. In fact, as Dr. Stopp notes, Francis' publications overlap one another chronologically so it is pointless to look for dramatic developments within this synthesis.

Above all, Dr. Stopp depicts Francis de Sales as a person, a person "one gets to know . . . in his books and in his letters ("Medieval Affinities," 162). The written word is the medium of a personal communication through which Francis (or a Teresa of Ávila, or a Cardinal Newman) are said to "come across to me as real people, known and loved" (*"Cor ad cor loquitur:* Newman and St. Francis de Sales," 183; cf. "Spanish Links: St. Francis de Sales and St. Teresa of Ávila," 172). Even when not stated in so many words, this observation is evidenced again and again—

so familiar has Dr. Stopp become with the people about whom she writes.

Parallel to the five characteristics of Dr. Stopp's portrayal of Francis de Sales, I would like to suggest five similarities which sketch a kind of self-portrait of Dr. Stopp herself. Do these similarities result from their personal empathy and friendship shared across the centuries? After all, Francis taught that friendship tends to produce a resemblance between friends. Or is it more simply an illustration of the colloquial expression "it takes one to know one"?

Whatever the reason, the reader will easily detect in these pages first of all a person who knows her own rootedness and who, by geographical, historical and literary references, reveals—all unintentionally—on what soil and in which cultural tradition these pages were written. Even though her parents came to England from different frontier regions of the Continent, Elisabeth had, as has been said, "a completely London childhood . . . in the medium of English" (*The Times*, London, 11 Nov. 1996).

While steeped in the history and literature of her own land, Dr. Stopp was also a scholar who had come to an intimate knowledge of the language and realities of seventeenth-century France and Savoy. She is thus uniquely able to draw parallels, make comparisons and point out historical details that few would suspect. At the same time her sense of history and her training in contemporary scholarship keeps her from "telescoping" epochs, for example, from concealing "the great divide between late medieval times and what we can already see as something like a 'modern' era" ("Medieval Affinities," 163). Nor does her estimation of Francis' modernity prevent her from saying that he would have experienced "astonishment and even bewilderment" ("The Context of Ecumenism," 197) to read parts of Vatican II's *Decree on Ecumenism* (1964). Thoroughly abreast of contemporary realities, Dr. Stopp provides a needed service for twentieth-century readers who are trying to understand Francis' time and our own.

Thirdly, Dr. Stopp is trained and gifted not only in history, but in literature as well. This background gives her a profound appreciation for the art of writing, for the way things are expressed. She admires this quality in Francis, as we have seen, and also in Jean Goulu, whose early biography of Francis is the only one which she would consider "a literary work in its own right": "And just because it is really a book, that is, a structural whole, it is in some sense worthy of Francis de Sales himself who was both saint and artist, and who proved in his own works that conscious literary shaping and a pleasing form can add very greatly to the effectiveness of spiritual teaching which draws hearts to the love of God ("The First Biography [1624]," 144). Here, above all, "it takes one to know one." Many authors of lives of the saints and popularizers of their teaching are oblivious to the literary element in their subjects (when it is to be found), and in their own writing. Not so Dr. Stopp. By recognizing the writing talent of Francis de Sales and by her own precise and pleasing way of translating him and of expressing herself, she proves herself in every sense worthy of her subject.

If Dr. Stopp has written about Francis de Sales' "essentially personal synthesis," it is because she has perceived and appreciated its shape, content and merit. While none of the essays here purports to spell out this synthesis in detail, it is clear from all her writings that she had a high estimation of what she has called his "inspired common sense" (see St. Francis de Sales, *Selected Letters*, 33-34) and an awareness of its relevance to the spiritual quest of many today, beginning no doubt with herself.

Finally, these observations relating Dr. Stopp's portrait of Francis to her own qualities lead one to realize that she herself comes across as a person one can get to know through the medium of these pages. That this impression emerges—not from personal letters and essays—but from precise research and scholarly lectures suggests the degree to which Dr. Stopp integrated her work and her life. This is why one can get to know her through this book. This is also why her research is never pointless, her scholarship never dull.

So let the reader be enriched by getting to know a British scholar of our time, even as she serves as a sure guide toward a much deeper and more personal knowledge of Francis de Sales and his time.

JOSEPH F. POWER, O.S.F.S.
DESALES RESOURCE CENTER
STELLA NIAGARA, NEW YORK

ACKNOWLEDGEMENTS

The essays and talks collected in this volume were written over a period of four decades, from the 1960s to the 1990s. Before her death in November 1996, Dr. Stopp prepared these texts for inclusion in this collection, doing minor rewriting in all of them.

Those texts which were not already adjusted to the American style of punctuation have been put in that format. For example, double quotation marks are used throughout (except for quotations within quotations), and commas and periods appear inside quotation marks. The format of endnotes has been made consistent throughout. In the essays, parenthetical references in the body of the texts have been eschewed in favor of all documentation appearing in the endnotes, whereas in the talks, a less formal style seemed appropriate, with endnotes being kept to a minimum.

Gratitude is expressed to the editors of *The Downside Review, Modern Language Review, The Month,* and *The Ransomer* for permission to republish the essays which originally appeared in these journals. Essays from *Salesian Studies* are republished with permission of the Provincial of the Wilmington-Philadelphia Province of the Oblates of St. Francis de Sales, which owned and published this quarterly journal, at Hyattsville, Maryland, from Spring 1962 to Autumn 1969.

François de Sales has always been known as "St. Francis de Sales" in the English spiritual tradition. This form has been used except where "François" seemed indicated, e.g., in the talk "Medieval Affinities: St. Francis of Assisi." St. Jeanne Françoise Frémyot de Chantal was known as "Madame de Chantal" even after her entry into religion and is now often called "St. Chantal," this surname having been adopted as a Christian name in France.

Dr. Stopp's translations of St. Francis de Sales' texts are her own, and all references to the original French texts, unless otherwise noted, are to *Oeuvres de Saint François de Sales*, Édition complète (the so-called "Annecy Edition"), 27 vols. (Annecy, 1892-1964), which henceforth are referred to as *Oeuvres*.

I am deeply grateful to Archbishop M. N. L. Couve de Murville of Birmingham (U.K.), a friend of Dr. Stopp of many years standing, for graciously accepting the invitation to write a foreword to this collection and to my confrère Father Joseph F. Power, O.S.F.S., Director of the DeSales Resource Center, Stella Niagara, New York, for generously contributing a preface. I also thank Dr. Terence O'Reilly, Professor of Spanish at University College Cork and Dr. Stopp's literary executor, and Father Power for their wise counsel on the final shape of this collection, as well as on various editorial points.

JOSEPH F. CHORPENNING, O.S.F.S.
EDITORIAL DIRECTOR
SAINT JOSEPH'S UNIVERSITY PRESS

LIST OF PLATES

1. Statue of Notre Dame de Bonne Déliverance, the Black Virgin of Saint-Étienne-des-Grès, before which St. Francis de Sales, as a student in Paris, prayed the Memorare and was delivered from the temptation to despair. Presently this statue is in the convent of the Sisters of St. Thomas of Villanova, Neuilly-sur-Seine.

2. C. de Mallery, *St. Teresa of Ávila*, engraving from Francisco de Ribera, *La vie de la Mère Thérèse de Jésus* (Paris, 1602).

3. Portrait of Madame de Chantal in 1607. Monastère de la Visitation de Saint-Pierre-d'Albigny (Savoie).

4. Martin Baes, *St. Francis de Sales*, engraving from the first English translation of the *Treatise on the Love of God* (Douay, 1630). (courtesy DeSales Center for Lay Spirituality, Washington, D.C.)

5. Portrait of Antonio Possevino, S.J.

6. Portrait of Antoine Favre

7. Emblem 48 from Adrien Gambart, *La Vie Symbolique du bienheureux François de Sales, compris sous le voile de 52 Emblèmes* (Paris, 1664). See p. below. (courtesy De Sales Resource Center, Stella Niagara, New York)

8. Certificate, in Cardinal Newman's hand, of Bishop Curtis' reception into the Catholic Church and conditional baptism (reproduced by permission of the Birmingham Oratory)

INTRODUCTION

St. Francis de Sales (1567-1622)

In a letter to a lady in Paris who had complained of his plain-speaking, Francis de Sales wrote: "I am quite prepared to admit that my letter was not without a certain rustic forthrightness, but need you take offense at this? You know very well the kind of country that produced me: can you expect delicate fruit from a mountain tree, and such a poor tree at that?" To the end of his life—this letter was written in 1621, the year before he died—Francis remained bound up with his homeland, the duchy of Savoy, the mountainous stretch of country placed between France, Switzerland and Italy, predominantly French in affinity but sharing to some extent in the culture of all three. He was born of an ancient noble family on 21 August 1567 at the castle of Thorens near Annecy, the little town on the lake which was the seat of the exiled bishop of Geneva and subject to the court of Piedmont at Turin. It was here that he spent most of his life; he was a "mountain tree," deeply rooted in the land of his origin, and it is against a background of ordered, stable hierarchy of traditional loyalty to his Church, his sovereign and his people that he must be seen and judged. His charm and gentleness, the aspects of his personality most apparent in his writing and therefore most generally stressed, form an incomplete picture; the vigour and tenacity, the uncompromising realism and common sense which characterize his race may too easily be overlooked. So too may the lifelong struggle which a man of exceedingly quick and strong reactions had to wage to overcome his naturally choleric temper. In the end the victory of grace was so complete in him that he now lives in the popular imagination as the most gentle of saints. But this judgement is superficial unless it is borne in mind that his was the gentleness of a God-given and yet hard-won integration, continually vitalized by the struggle of opposites which, as he himself says, lasted until the day of his death.

Francis de Sales was the eldest of thirteen children and as the heir to the family name he was destined to a career in the service of the state. He went to school at the Capuchin college at Annecy and when he was fifteen he was sent to study in Paris where he was inscribed in the arts faculty at the Jesuit College of Clermont. For the next six years he led the ordinary life of a student and nobleman of the time. He was accompanied by his own servant and by a strict priest tutor to whom he remained devoted and obedient throughout. He lodged in a hostelry close to the college in the Rue Saint Jacques, and apart from the courses in rhetoric and philosophy which he attended he also had lessons in fencing and dancing and became an accomplished horseman. The college was famous not only for its exemplary moral discipline at a time of great disorder but also for the excellence of its literary and humanistic studies, for the stress laid on outer stylistic form as well as on inner thought content. Through his grounding in Latin and Greek, his training in the art of reasoning and writing according to newly developed principles of philology and criticism, Francis was heir to all that was best in the Renaissance renewal of the University of Paris. As a writer he owes much to this training. The humanist substitution of a pleasing and conversational method of argument for the formal, rigid statement of the scholastics, of Plato and Cicero as models instead of Aristotle, coloured the whole bent of his mind and had a decisive influence on his prose style which was, in turn, to lay the foundations for the great prose of the classical period in French literature.

As a person coming from a small provincial town Francis gained his first insight into life in a great capital which was both the seat of a powerful government and a centre of culture and learning. He was a welcome visitor in the homes of the nobility among whom his father had connections. Although he was always rather reserved and quiet it appears that he had a great power of attraction and made many friends, for he was prepossessing both in manner and in appearance. He was tall and well built, his dress and general bearing handsome in the style of a nobleman of the period. Hoffbauer's portrait[1] shows a striking face framed by a high collar and set off by a black velvet cap decorated with a plumed white feather. The features are well shaped and regular, he has a determined mouth, finely marked eyebrows and large grey-blue eyes set wide apart and looking out into the world in a thoughtful and somewhat withdrawn manner. Indeed, there is a look almost as if of suffering in his face, perhaps a reflection of the spiritual crisis he went through in Paris when, for a time, overwork and a confusion of ideas on the matter of predestination made him feel that his soul was doomed to eternal separation from God. The torment of despair came to a sudden end as he knelt in prayer in Saint-Étienne-des-Grès saying the Memorare before an ancient statue of Mary. This personal experience of temptation on what was one of the chief points at issue in controversy with the Calvinists of Savoy undoubtedly helped to equip him in a special way for his work later on.

In the spring of 1588 he went back to Savoy for the first time in six years and after a holiday at home among the mountains he took the road again with his tutor and servant to go to Italy, to the University of Padua, for his higher legal studies. Three years later he took a brilliant doctorate in law and in the same year, a combination not unusual at the time, a doctorate in theology. Throughout this period Francis had been reading theology over and above his other studies and, as it were, on sufferance, as his father saw no need for this. Knowing what a blow it would be to him Francis had kept his religious vocation a secret from all except his mother. But it had been developing steadily from his boyhood days and he had only continued with his legal studies in a spirit of obedience while his heart was elsewhere. On his return from Padua he managed to enlist his mother's help and gradually accustom Monsieur de Boisy to the idea of his eldest son's ordination to the priesthood. The situation at home improved a little when an influential member of the family, himself a priest, secured for Francis the position of provost to the cathedral chapter of Geneva. This was the first step towards the bishopric, and while it pleased the father, it mortified the son who considered himself completely unfitted for such rapid preferment. After making over to his younger brother his rights of family succession and after a further period of study at home he was ordained. He celebrated his first mass on 21 December 1593 at Annecy.

The bishop, himself a man of deep spirituality, recognized his provost's capacity and extraordinary spiritual gifts and did the best thing possible for him at this stage: he appointed him to the hardest task his diocese had to offer, that of mission priest in charge of the Chablais. This was the district near the lake of Geneva which had recently been restored to Savoy but had become completely Calvinist during sixty years of alien occupation. Geneva itself whose name the see still bore, was hostile territory and the bishop and his representatives could only go there at the risk of imprisonment or even of life itself. It was a tough assignment for a young and inexperienced priest of twenty-six.

When Francis went there early in 1594, helped for the first few weeks by his priest cousin, there was not a single priest left in the area and only a handful of Catholics who had managed somehow to cling to their faith without the help of the Mass and the sacraments. At first Francis lived in a fortress garrisoned by the Duke of Savoy's soldiers, worked to some extent under their protection under conditions of intolerable hardship and poverty, ridiculed, persecuted, attacked even physically, saying Mass day by day in icy, half-ruined churches, preaching to empty pews. He persevered almost against hope. By the time he left his post four years later, after a triumphal celebration of the Forty Hours devotion to the Blessed Sacrament in the church at Thonon, attended by the Duke and a papal legate, the majority of the inhabitants had returned to the Church. It was a triumph of faith and fortitude but also of practical organizing capacity of a high order backed by expert legal knowledge. This hard apprenticeship brought Francis into contact with the realities of life, giving his spirituality a basis of realism and rock-like strength.

His missionary activity also led to the writing of his first book. He could not reach his people, especially the most educated and influential among them, by his preaching, so he set about writing, printing and distributing a series of regular broadsheets on points of Catholic doctrine, covering in time every aspect of the faith. The *Meditations on the Church* or *Controversies* (the title under which this work is usually known) are written, as Francis said in the introductory pamphlet by which he launched the series, not in a rich, ornate style but in the language and the manner natural to Savoy. He wrote trenchantly, confidently, neatly rounding off the clear statement of the profoundest truths with all the energy needed for polemics, but always charitably, already showing that secret gift of persuasion which characterizes all his later work and most especially his letters. He had the gift of moving the will without any showy eloquence but by relying on God in a clear and disciplined presentation of what he himself so ardently believed. "When I preach," he confided one day many years later to St. Vincent de Paul, "I feel something happening that I do not understand; I do not find the words as a result of my own efforts but by an impulse coming from God." The *Controversies* were not known in Francis' lifetime except by those to whom the leaflets were addressed over a period of years; but when in 1923 Pope Pius XI proclaimed St. Francis de Sales the patron of Catholic writers and journalists, he gave a high place to this work which differs so greatly in content and form, though not in purpose, from his later writings. So during the hard years in the Chablais he also served his apprenticeship as a writer. When he was a student he had written brilliant essays and theoretical exercises in controversy, as can be seen from some of the neat manuscript notebooks which have been preserved; but during the course of his missionary work he was for the first time faced with the practical tussle for the right word and phrase which was to persuade in real earnest and ultimately to save souls.

In 1598 Francis was nominated coadjutor to the See of Geneva, sent to Rome to represent his bishop in an *ad limina* visit to the Pope, and then in 1601 to Paris on a diplomatic mission concerning the restitution of ecclesiastical rights in territory which Savoy had yielded to Henry IV of France. The mission was not an unqualified success but during his six months' stay in the capital Francis gained high favour at court and in the city. He was in constant demand as a preacher and was asked to give the Lenten sermons at the Chapel Royal. "A rare bird, this Monsieur de Genève," said Henry IV who was famous for his apt summing-up of character, "he is devout and also learned; and not only devout and learned but at the same time a gentleman. A very rare combination." He became personally attached to Francis and tried to induce him to stay in Paris by offering a rich benefice; but though Francis appreciated all that Paris gave him in the course of his visit he was not to be tempted away from the comparative obscurity of his native Savoy. He gained experience, not always pleasant, of the conduct of affairs at the court and in high places, he got to know the devout life of the capital in its best aspect by meeting men and women of deep spirituality like Bérulle and Madame Acarie; he was admitted to their counsels on matters such as the introduction of St. Teresa's Carmelites into France and plans for the reforming of monasteries and convents. He was Madame Acarie's confessor for a time, was consulted on matters of conscience by persons at court and had his first experience of directing the souls of the kind of people he was to help later on. His first long letter of direction, to a superior who wanted to know how best to set about reforming her convent, dates from this time. It should perhaps be added that the morals at court reflected in general those of the king which were notoriously bad; and that religious life in communities was at a low ebb, though there was a strong counter movement of enlightened piety afoot, especially among the educated laity. The effect that Francis had on his contemporaries even at this early stage may therefore be called a personal triumph; it laid the foundations for his later work of spiritual direction among those who exerted influence over others, and also served as a long-term preparation for his founding of a new kind of religious order.

The bishop of Geneva died while Francis was on his way home from Paris. After a long retreat at the castle of Thorens, a time of great grace to which he often refers in his letters, he was consecrated bishop on 8 December 1602, the ceremony taking place, at his own wish in the village church where he had been baptized. He settled down quickly at Annecy where he was known and loved by all. He followed a rule which he had drawn up during his retreat, he lived without show but also without ostentatious poverty, he worked hard, gave as much time as he could to prayer, organized meetings and study or retreat days for his clergy. There was no seminary in his diocese and ordinations numbered about twenty a year; but during the twenty years of his tenure of office the average number rose to forty a year, an increase which is to be attributed almost entirely to his personal influence and organizing capacity. The bishop was available to all, "like a fountain," as he himself said, "in the marketplace." He spent hours in the confessional, choosing the box nearest to the entrance door, and he himself took over the children's catechism class which was soon attended, not only by every child in the town but by most of the devout adults, including his own mother, Madame de Boisy. He considered preaching one of his main responsibilities and wrote a short treatise on it in the shape of a letter to Monseigneur de Bourges, Madame de Chantal's brother. This admirable letter has not dated; it is concise, systematic and informative; it is also most revealing of the principles which guided Francis as a spiritual writer, that is, as one whose chosen instrument was the word, whether spoken or written. "Form, says the Philosopher, gives a thing being and life. Say wonderful things but say them badly and it amounts to nothing; say little and say it well, and it amounts to a great deal. How then ought we to talk when we are preaching? Beware of a lot of "quamquams" and the long periods of pedants, their gestures, expressions, movements, because this is what ruins preaching. Our speech should be unconstrained, noble, generous, straightforward, strong, devout, grave and deliberate. But how are we to achieve this? Quite simply by speaking with feeling and devotion, candidly and trustfully, by really being in love with the doctrine we are teaching and trying to get people to accept. The great art is to be art-less. The kindling power of our words must not come from outward demonstration but from within, not from the mouth but straight from the heart. Try as hard as you like but in the end only the language of the heart can reach another heart, while the sound of the tongue does not get past your listener's ear."

It was by the hidden power of this kind of preaching that Francis reached the heart that was to be most closely linked with his for the rest of his life. In 1604 he was invited to preach the Lenten sermons at Dijon where he stayed with the young archbishop to whom the letter was addressed. His sister had come up from the country to hear the sermons. Jane Frances Frémyot de Chantal was a young widow with four small children and a very difficult father-in-law in whose house she lived in humiliating circumstances. Her husband had been killed by one of his friends in a tragic hunting accident; after his death Jane Frances had given herself up to a life of austere piety under the direction of a confessor whose counsels inspired fear and anxiety rather than peace of mind. She turned to Francis for help, and following upon another meeting with her later that same year he agreed to undertake her direction. He directed her to sanctity.

In the vividly written contemporary life of Jane Frances by her secretary, Mother Chaugy,[2] we have some record of their annual meetings during the next six years before she came to settle at Annecy and found the first convent of their new order; but the real story of their relationship is told in Francis' letters to her. It was in trying to meet the spiritual need of a personality equal in calibre to his own and whom he loved that Francis found himself as a director, and because of the circumstances, as a letter-writer. During those early years he could still spare time to write letters peacefully. He wrote with care, entering at length into all difficulties, questions and scruples, generously pouring out all his gifts of heart and mind. Letters were highly prized in those days when people had few books and lived in the country remote from all opportunities for spiritual guidance or instruction. Madame de Chantal's friends at Dijon who had also placed themselves under Francis' direction, the Présidente Brûlart and her sister, the Abbess des Puis d'Orbe, had their share of letters at this time. From the beginning he can be seen in action with people of very different character and requirements.

Madame Brûlart was the type of young married woman who, having seen the spiritual light, at once felt she wanted to abandon house and home and a somewhat insensitive husband to enter the peace and solitude of Carmel. Her sister was a timid, perpetually discouraged and ailing nun whose desires were excellent but who lacked the grit necessary for really generous self-giving and for the difficult task of reforming her abbey. Madame de Chantal's brother had got his preferment much too young and he needed practical help, advice and spiritual guidance. Her father, a former president of the parliament of Dijon and an extremely able lawyer, was getting on in years and wanted to learn how to face old age and death. At home in Annecy Francis' young cousin, Madame de Charmoisy, coming from Paris and often returning to court, wanted to know how to combine a really devout inner life with the role she had to play in society and in the world.

Francis, who was himself as yet under forty, faced these varied spiritual claims upon him with calm equanimity, counselling prudently, advising without a trace of patronage, restraining or encouraging with equal wisdom and love. He referred his readers to books like the *Imitation of Christ*, the *Spiritual Combat* and the writings of Teresa of Ávila who had not long been beatified, but he could not point to anything which had been written specifically for devout lay people and their problems. His letters had in some sort to supply this deficiency. Together with essays on various spiritual topics which he called "Mémoire" or "Exercice" and which circulated among those he directed, the letters formed the basis of his first and most immediately successful work, the *Introduction to the Devout Life*. It was first published in 1608, carefully revised and then reprinted as often as forty times and translated into English, Italian, Latin, Spanish and German, all within his lifetime. Francis implied in his preface, and it has often been repeated, that the *Introduction* was based on the letters written to one particular person, later assumed to be Madame de Charmoisy; but quite apart from the fact that no letters to her have been preserved, it can be taken that the Philothea who is addressed throughout this book is really the type of all those who wanted to be devout this side of the cloister. This is a frame of mind which has not gone out of fashion and which accounts for the fact that the book is still a spiritual best-seller. Anyone who is familiar with this work and then turns to the letters cannot fail to identify the particular correspondents that Francis had more especially in mind at any given point of the *Introduction*, though much of it may also apply to anyone setting out resolutely on the way of devotion.

What was completely new in this book, apart from its whole conception, was the easy and unpontifical tone in which the bishop of Geneva explained the most serious subjects to Philothea. A complete programme of sanctity which in fact made the greatest possible demands on her was unfolded with conversational suppleness and in easily assimilated stages developing logically one out of the other. After an initial dedication to the devout life she was taught how to pray and make the best use of the sacraments. Then the practice of virtues proper to her state was explained to her and she was put on her guard against the temptations which beset her kind of life. Finally she was exhorted and encouraged to renew her resolutions to love God, and then to go cheerfully on her way. The careful arrangement and inner balance of the subject matter is reflected in the symmetry of the outer form, a series of brief chapters divided into five books. Whereas in the *Introduction* system prevails, though well disguised by informality, in the letters on which it is based there is the added immediacy which comes of realizing that a known and individual correspondent is being addressed in just the particular tone and terms which the situation requires. In later years when Francis was busier and more exhausted he would often simply refer his correspondents to the *Introduction* in the course of his letter, though he was always ready to explain personal variations where they were needed. Each Philothea and Philotheus remained an individual to him to the end. Indeed, it is astonishing that he did not repeat himself more often, considering how little, on the face of it, spiritual needs vary; but it is just this extra effort of love guided by imaginative insight of a very high order that distinguishes the letters of an artist who was also a saint.

In an indirect way he conjures up the portrait of all his correspondents. After his death Madame de Chantal destroyed all the letters she had written to him and which he had carefully kept and even annotated. The loss of one half of what would have made a unique spiritual correspondence may be considered tragic, but it does not need a very great effort of the imagination to reconstruct the nature and general tenor of her letters from Francis' own. She was ardent, generous and strong, inclined, at the beginning, to rush to extremes, exacting in the demands she made on herself though not on other people, untiring in her love and charity towards those in need, absolutely forthright and fearless in her dealings. She came of a family of distinguished lawyers and though she had little formal education and her spelling was highly erratic, she was a woman of great intelligence, able to express herself concisely and analyse in clear terms a thing as intangible as a spiritual state of mind. Francis himself commended her for this ability. She had charm, wit and was a shrewd judge of character, qualities which need not cause surprise in Madame de Sévigné's grandmother. Madame de Chantal's son, to whom Francis addressed one of his most famous letters, was the father of Marie de Rabutin-Chantal who became perhaps the most famous of all letter-writers.

Madame de Chantal responded whole-heartedly to Francis' direction which changed her inner life completely, freed it, not indeed from great trials which always remained, but from all excess, scruples and anxiety, leaving the way clear for the work of God's grace in her. She had dedicated her state of widowhood to God and wanted to leave the world as soon as her responsibilities to her children would allow it. In the same way as Francis had formulated a new type of spirituality of Christian humanism for those who remained in the world, so he created a new kind of religious congregation for Madame de Chantal and others of her kind who had a vocation for the religious life. On 6 June 1610 he founded the first convent of the Visitation of Holy Mary at Annecy with Madame de Chantal, Marie-Jacqueline Favre, Charlotte de Bréchard and one lay-sister, Jacqueline de Coste, a remarkable peasant woman whom he had met earlier on in the course of his mission work in Geneva. The congregation was contemplative, open to widows as well as to the usual kind of younger postulant but received people who might have been refused by a more austere order for reasons of health. The nuns led a simple, hidden life of prayer, not marked by any extremes of penance and austerity, following what Francis called "the way of simplicity." Until the second foundation was made at Lyons in 1615 the nuns did not take solemn vows, were not enclosed and used to go out to visit the sick. Whereas the Visitation then became entirely contemplative, the idea of nursing the sick, at that time unheard of for nuns who were thought of as strictly enclosed, was taken over by Francis' friend, St. Vincent de Paul, when he founded the Sisters of Charity. Francis had intended the visiting which was strictly limited in time and scope to be a help towards a healthy and balanced contemplative life and subordinate to it; for the main stress of the congregation was always on this. He yielded on this point to the conservatism of the archbishop of Lyons who considered that the presence of unenclosed nuns in his town would lead to scandal and all kinds of difficulties.

Francis was now faced with the task of directing a new institute, a contemplative community, and for the help of those who had left the world to lead a more perfect life of prayer he wrote his *Treatise on the Love of God*. Although the book only appeared in 1616 the plan of the *Treatise* had been made and work begun on it before the *Introduction* was actually published in 1608. There was no break or sudden transition in Francis' writing activity, but the book reflects a considerable change and development in those for whom he was writing and probably also in himself. As he witnessed the mystical life growing in the Visitandines and saw it as it were concretely and objectively outside himself, the things that were going on in his own soul gradually grew ripe for formulation. Francis saw the mystical life as the active love of God unfolding in the soul. He therefore set himself to study—in the Scriptures, in the Fathers, in St. Thomas, in the "very learned ignorance," as he called it, of St. Teresa of Ávila, in other writers of his own time, but above all in his own soul and in those whom he directed at Annecy—the relationship of love between the human person and God. This led him to examine Christian morals systematically in the light of love increasing in the soul, and to describe the practical effects of growing love on prayer, on human relationships, on daily life. The "mountain-tree" of this unique personality was firmly rooted in its native earth; and in the same way Francis, the theologian, set the structure of his mystical theology firmly upon the basis of ascetical theology, thus producing a synthesis of great originality. Inspired intuition is held in balance by sound, logical thought, resulting in a kind of *Summa* of divine love. Not that he claimed to have said anything new. All he did, perhaps all that great discoverers in the realm of the spiritual life ever do, was to combine old truths in a new way.

The book was written for Théotime this time, for any soul that is already devout and wants to advance in the love of God. Although the personal form of address is not lacking, one has the impression that the basic literary pattern is no longer that of the letter but that of the more discursive colloquy, the exchange of ideas which took place in the Visitation parlour or in the convent orchard overlooking the lake and the mountains. And here Francis was no longer only the guide and teacher, but the learner together with other learners. Many of the ideas in the *Treatise* do still find their place in letters and were originally formulated there, but on the whole there is a change of atmosphere in the letters from about 1610 onwards. Regular correspondence with Madame de Chantal had ceased though there was a constant interchange of notes between the bishop's palace and the convent, and there were letters of greater length when she went away to make foundations or when either was ill. Théotime gets fewer letters than Philothea did, and he is asked instead to pick up his copy of the *Treatise* and to read a chapter of it if his affection for his spiritual father sometimes makes him long to have a letter which seems to be slow in coming. But of course other Philotheas come to take the place of the earlier ones and they are treated with equal love and respect for their uniqueness as personalities; only there is greater simplicity, a more insistent emphasis on the one thing needful in which he himself was immersed.

Not that there was ever a clear-cut distinction between the ascetical and the mystical in Francis, for indeed throughout his life the two run side by side and merge into one another, though one kind of emphasis may appear more prominent at various stages and ages. It is one of the characteristic features of Francis de Sales' spiritual correspondence as a whole that no sharp dividing line exists at any time between one "stage" and another. It is only that a different atmosphere is sensed, a slight shifting of emphasis, often within one and the same letter. It would in any case be mistaken to look for theories of the mystical as such in letters which were dictated by changing personal and practical requirements. The counterpart to the *Introduction* on a different level is rather to be found in the *Spiritual Conferences*. These have been preserved in transcriptions made by the Visitandines of talks given in answer to specific questions and on special occasions. It remains true that everything Francis said or wrote during these last few years of his life bears the imprint of his own constantly deepening love of God. There is an ever greater simplicity, an intensity of purpose which is reflected in the very rhythm of the sentences he writes as his life draws to a close.

There were still years of toil and suffering to come but his heart remains as it were enclosed at the Visitation, leading the hidden life of prayer which he longed for increasingly as the years went on. The affairs of his diocese remained excessively burdensome and intricate, his relations with his sovereign, a suspicious and unreasonable man, were always difficult. Within his own lifetime Francis supervised, through Madame de Chantal, the foundation of thirteen other Visitation convents in various parts of France. He suffered from continual ill-health, from calumny, from an ever increasing load of business and correspondence. For business letters he employed a secretary, but right to the end every letter of direction—and there were times when he wrote fifty or more letters a day of one kind or another—was written in his own hand, in his upright, beautifully formed italic characters, legible and vital right up to the very last letter of all. In the spring of 1617, and again in the following year, he made new contacts at Grenoble when he preached the Lenten sermons there. Each Philothea of these later days received letters which entered into her problems, little and great, with the same inexhaustiblepatience as of old, but it was now also possible for the director to harness some of the new-found ardour to furthering the spread of the Visitation. This was an excellent practical object which drew off usefully a good deal of spiritual energy from the first immediate object of its projection, Francis himself.

No one can read his letters without being deeply struck by the untiring generosity with which he received the affection he inspired and with which he returned it as soon as he saw that anyone sincerely wanted to serve God through the help of his direction. It lay in the nature of things that these people were mostly women, for as he himself said in a letter to Madame de Chantal from Grenoble that same year: "It is the ladies who excel in devotion in this town, for here like everywhere else men leave the cares of the household and the practice of piety to their women-folk." But the letters to the Duc de Bellegarde, one of the greatest statesmen of his time, are only an instance among many others that Francis' affections went out equally to all. As soon as any person, whatever the difficulties of his or her temperament, is judged to lie in real earnest in the desire to lead a devout life, Francis adopts a new child into the overgrowing household of his heart. A man is forthwith addressed and really becomes *mon très cher fils*, a woman *ma très chère fils*, while the bishop himself asks to be called without ceremony by the name he held dearest *mon père*. As one can see in the autographs the words *ma très chère* are written, as time goes on, in one connected movement of the pen and become a single concept; no one could be his child without being very dear to him. Nor is this an empty formula; he means it and he repeats the personal form of address often throughout the letter to the beloved son or daughter vividly present to his mind. He was not afraid of love or of allowing himself to be used as a channel for the love of God.

In November 1618 he went to Paris in the suite of Cardinal Maurice of Savoy who was charged with negotiating the marriage between Christine of France and the Prince of Piedmont. Madame de Chantal also went there to see to the newly founded Visitation convent. He spent practically a whole year in the capital, a time of incessant labour, attending at court, preaching almost daily, receiving visitors and counselling all who called upon his help. His most remarkable friendship at this time was no doubt that with Vincent de Paul to whom he entrusted the direction of the Visitation and of Madame de Chantal after his death, and who became one of the witnesses at the first process of canonization in 1628. "His ardent fervour," said Vincent, "shone through his public preaching as well as his ordinary conversation. When I thought about his words afterwards I admired them so deeply that I felt sure he was the best living portrait of the Son of God on earth. I remember thinking again and again: How good You must be, my dear God, since Monsieur de Genève who is but Your creature is so wonderfully good and kind." This was the sort of impression he made on people and none seemed able to resist his spell. His letters from Paris reveal a man entirely carried by God's love and united to Him, a man who was making a last great effort in the face of exhaustion to meet an infinite number of demands. From the point of view of his correspondence his most important contact was that with Angélique

Arnauld, the young Abbess of Port Royal who placed herself under his direction and enlisted his help in the reform of her convent. She was an extraordinarily gifted woman but tempestuous and self-willed; this is only too evident by implication in the letters which Francis wrote to her. He made a supreme effort of charity to save her from herself, for he loved and admired her and predicted great things for her if only she could learn to let God have His way. He cannot have been wrong in thinking her the kind of person who had it in her to rise to great heights, but the opposite tendency was also there to balance this and he was well aware of it. Had Francis lived and had she been able to enter the Visitation as she wished, she might never have been deceived by Jansenism.

The cardinal's suite followed the court to Tours and spent some time there. Francis arrived home towards the end of the year 1620, having once more refused all honours and benefices, even the succession to the see of Paris. He went about his work in Annecy with as much zeal as ever, though with increasing difficulty and with an ever greater longing to retire, to write at leisure, to fix his mind wholly on God. The next autumn, one crisp September day, he went up into the mountains to bless a sanctuary, a hermitage where the holy founder of the Abbey of Talloires had ended his days in solitude. After the ceremony, as Francis stood looking out over the landscape he loved, the fields and valleys of the foothills, the snow-capped mountains beyond the lake, he told the abbot how he longed to leave the heat and burden of the day to another, to live in a solitude of this kind, "serving God with his rosary and his pen." At the beginning of that year his brother John had been appointed his coadjutor. He had some help from him but he also had the task of training a successor, a man of uncertain temper to whom he always showed unalterable good humour.

In the autumn of 1622 Francis joined the court of Savoy for a meeting with the court of France at Avignon and later at Lyons, where Louis XIII conferred with the Prince of Piedmont and Christine. Francis knew when he left Annecy that he would not return. At Lyons he refused all offers of sumptuous lodgings and chose to stay in the gardener's cottage in the grounds of the Visitation convent a little way out of the town. All the hours he could spare from official duties were spent with the nuns and it was there he saw Madame de Chantal for the last time. She had been away from Annecy in Paris and making foundations elsewhere; she had not seen him for three years. She had hoped that they would talk as of old of spiritual matters, of her own state of soul and of his; but he saw fit to confine their long conversation entirely to practical administrative affairs concerning the Visitation. As soon as all business was settled he asked her to leave at once for a visit to the convent at Belley which needed her presence. No personal word passed between them, though for the whole of the month that Francis spent at Lyons his cottage was open to all the great and little people who cared to consult him. His last letter, written on Christmas Eve, was an appeal for a poor man who was out of work. To the end the pattern of his life remained the same, one of complete self-abnegation and of perfect self-giving. On 27 December he had a seizure and he died the next day on the Feast of the Holy Innocents, at the age of fifty-five. According to his own wish he was buried in the church of the first Visitation convent in Annecy which also became the resting place of Jane Frances de Chantal in 1641.

NOTES

1. A reproduction of this portrait may be found on the cover of Antoine Dufournet's *La jeunesse de Saint François de Sales, 1567-1602 (Paris, 1942)*.

2. Mère Françoise-Madeleine de Chaugy, *Mémoires sur la Vie et les Vertus de Sainte Jeanne-Françoise Frémyot de Chantal*, in vol. 1 of *Vie et Oeuvres de Sainte Chantal (Paris, 1893)*.

CHRONOLOGY

1567.......................... 21 August: François Bonaventure de Sales
born at Thorens in Savoy

1575.......................... To school at Annecy

1578.......................... 20 September: He receives clerical tonsure

1580-88.................... At Clermont College, Paris

1588-91.................... Legal and theological studies at Padua

1592.......................... He returns to Savoy

1593.......................... Provost of the Cathedral Chapter of Geneva;
ordination on 18 December at Annecy

1594-98.................... Missionary in the Calvinist Chablais region
on the southern banks of Lac Léman

1598.......................... He visits Rome and is appointed coadjutor
to the Bishop of Geneva resident at Annecy

1600.......................... *Defense of the Standard of the Holy Cross*

1601.......................... Death of his father, Monsieur de Boisy

1602.......................... In Paris at the court of Henri IV on behalf
of his bishop. On 8 December he is
consecrated Bishop of Geneva at the village
church of Thorens

1604.......................... He preaches the Lenten sermons at Dijon
and meets Madame de Chantal

1609........................ *Introduction to the Devout Life*

1610........................ 1 March: Death of his mother

1610........................ 6 June: Visitation founded at Annecy with Madame de Chantal

1616........................*Treatise on the Love of God*

1618-19..................... He is in Paris for the marriage of the Prince of Piedmont with Christine of France. Paris Visitation founded

1622........................ He crosses the Alps to go to Pignerolo and Turin. In November he sets out on his last journey in the suite of the Prince Cardinal of Savoy

1622........................ 28 December: He dies of a stroke in Lyons

1623........................ 24 January: Funeral at Annecy

1627........................ First canonization inquiries at Annecy, later at Orléans and in Paris

1633........................ His cause postponed

1641........................ Death of Madame de Chantal

1661........................ Beatification of Francis de Sales

1665........................ 19 April: Canonization

1767........................ Canonization of Jane Frances de Chantal

1877........................ St. Francis de Sales declared a Doctor of the Church

1923........................ St. Francis de Sales declared Patron of Writers and Journalists

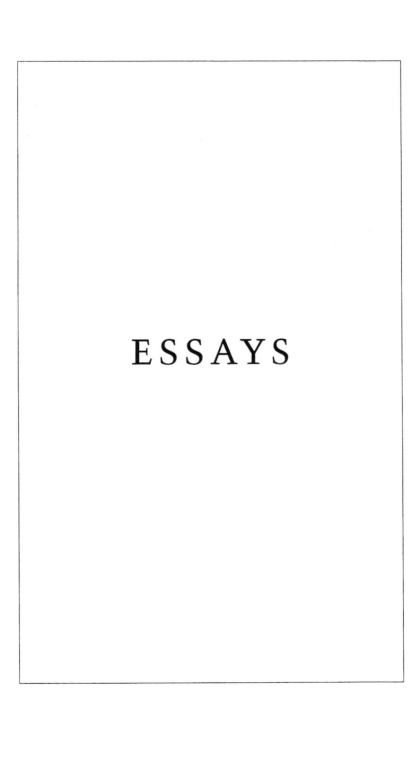

ESSAYS

I

St. Francis de Sales at Clermont College:
A Jesuit Education in Sixteenth-Century Paris

Francis de Sales, accompanied by his tutor, Monsieur Déage, a steward and a personal servant, set out for Paris sometime in the late summer of 1580 or 1581 so as to reach the city in time for the opening of the scholastic year at the beginning of October. Sons of noble houses in Savoy were not allowed to leave the country for their education without the duke's permission. The official pass had already been obtained together with that for his three elder cousins who had left Brens for Paris two or three years earlier. It was dated 1579.[1] Before setting out, Francis was given his sword, the sign of his standing, and he himself chose a personal motto, the one which he kept all his life: *non excidet*, a prayer, the powerful and complex word "excidere" implying: "may he not fail in his attempt, perish, be lost." It was his already characteristic response to the general atmosphere of adulation and high hope which surrounded his setting out.

The journey took about a fortnight, partly on horseback and partly by boat along the Rhône and the Loire, the great towns through which they passed being Lyons, Bourges and Orléans. The road from Orléans to Paris was the only stretch of highroad in France which was paved all the way at that time, and it was along this ancient Roman highway leading straight to the Quartier Latin on the left bank of the Seine that the travelers entered Paris through the gate of Saint Jacques. The college to which Francis was to go, that of Clermont, was situated in this same rue de Saint Jacques not far from the gate, and the house where he lived at first, the Hôtel de la Rose Blanche, was almost opposite. Adjoining it was the Sorbonne, the college which had given its name to the whole theological faculty of the University of Paris. The road sloped more steeply to the river than it does now. Steps led down the hill, and on either side of the highroad, behind the shops clustered onto the main academic buildings, narrow alleyways led from one college to another, a network of paths replacing the older ways which had traversed the vineyards once situated on the Mont Saint Geneviève in Gallo-Roman and Merovingian times.

No sooner had Francis ungirded his sword in the hostelry where the party had put up on arrival than he at once asked to be directed to the college of the Jesuit fathers, saluted the prefect of studies and made his petition to be taken on as a student. He was well received and at once liked.[2] Clermont College had been the boy's own independent choice, and this was the first time that he had broken away from the paths decreed by family counsel. His cousins had gone to the College of Navarre, a short walk from Clermont and situated where the École Polytechnique is now. It had seemed a matter of course to Monsieur de Boisy that Navarre was the right choice; for Savoyard noblemen, Navarre followed Annecy rather like King's College followed Eton. It was among the most aristocratic of all, the academy par excellence of the French nobility; it was just what Francis' father wished for his eldest son who was to make the right contacts. But it was also true, as Francis had found out from older friends and possibly from his cousin Louis who had an outlook similar to his own, that there was much irregular, even debauched living at this and other colleges, that Clermont was one of the few places where teachers and pupils were not morally suspect and where decent, devout behavior was the rule.[3] This college too had its share of students from among the nobility, and quite apart from that Francis was attracted by what he had heard of Jesuit teaching methods.

The "Company" was then in its first vigor. The founder had only been dead some twenty-five years when Francis went to Paris. Jesuit schools had spread rapidly all over Europe, and the particular program of religious humanism which they made their aim was a talking point even in Savoy. Chambéry, the former capital of the duchy, had a Jesuit college. Francis, not wanting to affront his father and his uncle, the head of the family, felt that a considerable amount of tact was called for in explaining his preference. He put the whole thing to his mother, telling her too of his real fear of being influenced by his own strong impulses and by bad example. "Tu es inclin au mal," he had said to himself.[4] She understood his fear, then spoke "so persuasively and effectively" to her husband that he too began to see the point and finally gave his parental blessing for Clermont.

In his speech of thanks to the Senate of the University of Padua after his doctorate was conferred on him ten years later, Francis spoke with affection of Paris as a most flourishing university. "It was here," he said, "that I first applied myself to the humanities and then to philosophy in all its aspects; and my task was made all the easier and more fruitful because this university was so addicted, as one might say, to philosophy and theology, that its very walls and rooftops seem to join in philosophical discussion."[5] An immensely lively and stimulating atmosphere had for centuries been the hallmark of the University of Paris which had, in the past, attracted the finest intellects of Europe. The fourteenth and fifteenth centuries saw the peak of its reputation; a certain decline set in during the course of the following century when intellectual leadership in Europe had gone to Italy, the country least disturbed by the Reformation, or rather, where the Renaissance had to some extent played the role of the Reformation. From about the middle of the sixteenth century the decline had been arrested to some degree by the foundation of the Collège Royal[6] directly by the crown, and then by the more gradual emergence of Clermont, dating from 1563. It was the aim of both these colleges to convey and extend the best humanist tradition of the Renaissance, and in the case of Clermont, the object was expressly to christianize the humanism, that is, to apply the principles and spirit of the Counter Reformation to the upbringing and education of the young, making the two great pagan cultures of the ancient world serve the faith. What did this mean in practice, and what was the form of training which Francis de Sales received at Clermont for the next eight years?

We are told that first of all, for three or four years, he continued the humanities which he had already begun at Annecy and which led up to rhetoric. In 1584 at the age of seventeen he was promoted to philosophy, remaining in this class for the last four years of his stay in Paris. At the end of this course he was pronounced "proficient in the humanities" but had no degree on paper as the Jesuits in France were at that time forbidden to give official academic degrees. This was a merely formal prohibition which deceived no one. During the last years of Francis' stay he also attended theology lectures at the Sorbonne together with his tutor, himself a student of theology, whose notebooks he in any case read throughout the years, avidly absorbing this and every other form of knowledge which presented itself. Theology was, however, a graduate field, together with law, medicine, and music, this being the traditional arrangement of subjects at the medieval university which was still current in Europe throughout the sixteenth and a part of the seventeenth century. At Clermont Francis had not yet begun to specialize officially.

It is commonplace among the biographers to say that as a writer he owed a great deal to his humanist education at Clermont, but to substantiate this we are given little more than the names of his classes and of the men, well known in their time but now long forgotten, who were his teachers. We are told that he learnt how to write and to speak eloquently. It seems worthwhile to take a rather closer look at the curriculum he followed during these seven or eight years, to see how his training was organized and how its general spirit and even to some extent its concrete detail might have influenced a future writer.

Francis was one of 1200 pupils at Clermont. The number had risen to 1500 by the time he left,[7] and although many of these boys became statesmen and ecclesiastics of note, very few are remembered as writers. It is true that Molière and Voltaire followed Francis de Sales in the same school later on, but this is not mentioned as proof that the Clermont form of teaching automatically produced results. Just as Milton as a poet and writer is, however, unthinkable without the background of seventeenth-century scholastic learning at Cambridge, much though he personally disapproved of it, so Francis de Sales' whole cast of mind and the nature and structure of his literary work could not have come into being without the *Ratio Studiorum* of this early Jesuit school. Because of the highly centralized nature of the Company and its systematic documentation at every stage, there is ample evidence about the detail of the curriculum followed at Clermont in Francis' time.[8] It will be described in outline insofar as it may be considered relevant to the study of Francis de Sales as a writer.

The official foundation of the Society of Jesus goes back to 1540. When St. Ignatius Loyola died in 1556, there were already more than seventy schools and seminaries, and by the time Clermont was opened in 1563, developing into a school from a house of studies for Jesuits working at the Sorbonne, the plan of education at the school already had a systematic shape. The college was named after the Bishop of Clermont, Guillaume du Prat, who had housed Ignatius' students in his own home and had left money for them to buy another property after his death. This was the Hôtel de Langres in the rue de Saint Jacques, a fifteenth-century building of severe aspect with high, forbidding walls toward the street but unexpectedly pleasant within, having a large court and a garden with a well of its own. The establishment of the college aroused immediate opposition on the part of the Sorbonne and of parliament; education there was free, as laid down by the founder, and from the beginning these excellent new teachers attracted large numbers. Their sober, strict way of life and the general sense of ordered discipline and hard work amounted to an implied criticism of what was going on in most of the neighboring establishments in the Quartier Latin. The Jesuits were forbidden to call the school by their own name and so they adopted that of their benefactor. In the seventeenth century it enjoyed the high favor of Louis XIV and was named after him. Remodeled considerably, the building still stands in the same spot, and is still one of the most renowned schools in Paris, the Lycée Louis le Grand, now run by the state.

It was never the intention of the Jesuits to be innovators or revolutionaries in education; they simply wanted to ensure sound traditional instruction on scholastic lines. As the administrative center of the Company was in Rome, and many of the earliest members were Italian, they were naturally influenced by the Italian court and city schools which were in a leading position in Europe. Their humanist ideal was that laid down by Quintilian; a truly educated man was one who could express himself with sincerity, readiness and persuasiveness on the entire circle of knowledge, that is, classical, or Greek and Latin knowledge.[9] For there was no other. The Jesuits absorbed this basic ideal into their general aim of preparing educated apostles of Christ's kingdom on earth by means of a harmonious development of intellect and will, mind and spirit. Apart from the overall spiritual training, the means by which this was achieved was the teaching of the humanities, a training of the literary faculties. The student's reasoning powers were developed and his mind furnished with knowledge so that by applying logic to facts he was in a position to express his thoughts as accurately and perfectly as possible. Expression and communication were the final aim. The ethical and moral aspects of this training ensured that what was expressed and communicated served, ultimately, to extend the sphere of Christian influence.

As it seemed essential to the Company to coordinate instruction in its various schools, a number of provisional schemes were drawn up from the beginning. This resulted in the first printed plan, or the *Ratio Studiorum*, published in Rome in 1586, that is, while Francis was actually at Clermont. It was worked out by a committee of six, the representative for France, it is pleasant to remember, being a Scotsman, James Tyrie (1543-97), who had taught at Paris. After criticism had been submitted from every school in Europe, and after further suggestions from experts in the leading Roman College itself, the *Ratio* was redrafted and given two further editions in 1591 and 1599. The alterations concerned detail and local variations; the essential lines of instruction were unchanged from the time Francis was at Clermont.

The humanistic curriculum was divided into five main sections, three lower, or grammar classes, followed by the humanities class and finally by rhetoric. Philosophy, the next class, was already a distinct subject though not yet a graduate specialized field. Graduate studies were not represented at Clermont but they were professed at the Jesuit universities of Pont-à-Mouson in Lorraine, and at Ingolstadt in Bavaria. The syllabus of the *Ratio* had developed out of the older scholastic educational scheme of the seven liberal arts arranged as the Trivium (grammar, dialectics, rhetoric) and the Quadrivium (arithmetic, geometry, music, astronomy). This still pertained in the universities unaffected by humanist changes, and constituted the arts faculty which was only preparatory to the three main ones, theology, law, and medicine. In the Jesuit schools no age groups were fixed; promotion depended entirely on progress, but a boy could reckon to reach rhetoric by the age of about seventeen, as Francis did, and then three or four years in philosophy. He was not considered ready to specialize before the age of twenty-one.

It would be true to say that his preparatory, non-specialist studies on the Italian Jesuit model were exceptionally long and thorough, which was of the greatest possible advantage to a man whose life was to be spent largely in speaking, preaching and writing. The fostering of these capacities was the great aim of this system. Latin and Greek served as the medium through which the pupil learnt the use of his own mother tongue, at that time not yet considered a sufficiently developed and cultured medium for the purpose of actual training. In every other way the vernacular had already been firmly established by the Renaissance.

The object of the grammar classes was to achieve accurate simple Latin, to be written and spoken *proprie et pure et absque vitio*. Latin was begun with an actual grammar composed by one of the Jesuits; in the middle and upper sections of grammar there was Vives' *De Exercitatione Linguae Latinae* (also used at the English court at that time). A beginning was made on the easier letters of Cicero and on his *De Amicitia* or *De Senectute*, and there might be a selection from Terence or from Virgil's *Eclogues*. In the humanities at the age of fourteen or fifteen, Greek was begun. There was greater concentration on matters of style which was to be *copia et elegantia*, and there was also more poetry, for instance, the third book of Horace's *Odes,* the *Ars Poetica*, Ovid's *De Tristibus* and *De Ponte*, while Cicero's letters, together with Caesar's Gallic Wars still formed the staple diet. To this was added, for light relief, Erasmus' guide on letter writing, *De Conscribendis Epistolis.* For Greek there was above all Aesop's book of fables, also Aristophanes' *Pluto*, and other works, carefully edited in the interests of decency. In fact, Greek was under a slight cloud in Paris as a whole towards the end of the sixteenth century, since it was closely identified with the name Erasmus who was considered theologically suspect as a forerunner of Luther. There was still more Greek at Clermont than elsewhere in Paris except at the Collège Royal, but it remains true to say that Greek appears to have had little real influence on Francis de Sales. It never became a part of his mental horizon in the way that Latin did, and what does remain of Greek culture in his works reached him largely through the medium of Latin. The aim in the rhetoric class was *eloquentia perfecta contendo esse Ciceroni aequalem*, the concept of *eloquentia* having a far wider connotation than our equivalent idea of surface polish. It embraced the whole man and his general culture by which he could express and put across to the world the spiritual and intellectual thought content of his mind. The pupil now proceeded to Cicero's orations, to Quintilian's works on oratory, to further historical authors in both Latin and Greek. Lucian's dialogues also found a place as a form of relaxation from sterner studies.[10]

In philosophy there was a radical change, as here the subject matter became for the first time an end in itself; and in order to help the student to deal consciously with the influx of new material, that is, with Aristotelian science, mathematics and ethics, he was introduced to the systematic organization of thought by means of logic. He was actually taught how to think and be aware of the mechanism of his thought process, to link his judgments into a sequence by means of analogy, relation, and especially by syllogisms where a new conclusion followed naturally from a previously known factor common to two earlier statements. Logic in the first philosophy year was paired with the elements of Euclid, especially geometry, and with introductory physics, this not being the current narrower field of the properties of matter and energy, but the study of natural phenomena in general, such as zoology, biology, plant life as well as cosmology. This last was the theory of the universe being an ordered whole governed by definite laws and by a supreme lawgiver, God. The second philosophy year saw the continuation of mathematics and science and the beginning of metaphysics, that is, especially psychology as the study of the relationship between soul and body, the way in which the intellect works and the method of operation of the five senses. Metaphysics in the final year was continued by the study of moral philosophy and ethics, this being not so much distinctions between right and wrong, or moral rules, but the discovery of what form of life is conducive to man's highest good, what virtues lead to his greatest happiness and fulfillment. Aristotle's *Organon, Physics* and *Metaphysics* were read in the Latin translations of Italian humanist scholars who had given his treatises these names; they were studied in conjunction with their Christian exegesis and commentary, the *Summa* of St. Thomas Aquinas.[11]

By what methods was this comprehensive scheme of literary education implemented at Clermont, and what was the actual aspect of the lessons and lectures Francis de Sales attended for these seven or eight years? The most striking thing about the practical side of Jesuit teaching was that although the system was supple and could be adapted in its detail to local conditions, nothing about the main outline and method was left to chance. It was a judicious blend of actual teaching and of training the pupil to learn on his own. There were five hours of class instruction every day, divided equally between morning and afternoon, the actual points of time being fixed by local custom. In Paris the first lesson began at seven o'clock with the *praelectio* by the teacher. This was the direct predecessor of the French *explication de texte*, and popularizing this humanist method was one of the most notable contributions which the Company made to education in general. The teacher first read aloud the new subject matter, for example, one of Cicero's letters or part of an Eclogue of Virgil, then commented on the grammatical structure, the literary content and form, in accordance with the models given by the *Ratio* at several stages of knowledge. In the humanities and rhetoric the *praelectio* dealt more with ideas and the manner of expressing thought, with allusions, figures of speech and mythological references, differentiating between synonyms and accounting for the author's choice of vocabulary. Greater emphasis was placed on erudition, but the general aim remained as before, to teach the pupil how to study, understand and make practical use of a text for the enriching of his own thought and style: *imitatio est anima praelectionis.*

In the lower classes a little French was allowed, but the general rule for all question and answer in class was Latin. The actual work of learning followed on the *praelectio* with the teacher calling on pupils to repeat in their own words certain aspects of what had been explained, to translate, to read out from their notebooks the personal comments made while the explanation was going on. As the class might be very large, anything up to about two or three hundred at Clermont in Francis' time, it was then divided into two main groups called Spartans and Carthaginians, to encourage a spirit of healthy emulation. Each camp was subdivided into units of ten in charge of a bright pupil who was called a decurion and who functioned for only a month at a time. It was his duty to repeat and memorize the text with his team for the next hour while the teacher walked round helping, testing and, in the last half hour, hearing the assembled decurions. In the afternoon skillful questioning about the morning's work helped to settle the new material and then there might be written work or else a further brief *praelectio*. Memorizing well-understood passages of Latin and Greek was considered important, not only to sharpen the memory itself but to provide the pupil with a store of words and phrases and to give him a sense of rhythm and style for his own writing. The written work, Latin and Greek essays or verses on set topics, for instance, a proverb, some historical event, the virtues and vices, was a regular and new feature of the teaching designed to arouse mental activity and reflection: *ut excitetur ingenium*. Independently organized material laid before the tutor was the forerunner of the present weekly essay at the older universities. Essays alternated with oral practice, that is, with a declamation on some subject, or else with recitation of memorized matter where much attention was paid to voice-production, pronunciation, gesture and stance. On Saturday, which was a kind of field day, there were contests between the two camps and this took the form of a survey of the week's new work. The daily brief period of catechism was also revised at the weekend.

To help the boys in their written work they were instructed from the beginning in how to keep a *copia verborum*, or commonplace book, of their own, arranging it systematically under headings. These books were an important instrument of humanist teaching. They abound even now in MSS in Oxford and Cambridge college libraries,[12] and they account to a large extent for what is to us the astonishing allusiveness of seventeenth-century writing in general. The early habit of keeping a *copia verborum* is certainly of importance for understanding Francis de Sales' manner of writing: he continued throughout his life to read and write with an eye on his notebook of "similitudes" and other quotable material.

Great emphasis, too, was placed on good, clear speaking, and this was further fostered by the famous and novel Jesuit practice of producing school plays in Greek and Latin on sacred or classical subjects.[13] The idea came not from Italy but from Portugal, which also invented the system of decurions in school. At Clermont drama was not prominent till the following century when it became a vogue of considerable importance for the French classical theater. It may be said in passing that both the Corneille brothers were pupils of the Company's school at Rouen. Clermont produced a play on Herod in 1579, just before Francis' time, and no others are noted in the records though it is likely that there were small informal productions. Ceremonial prize-givings with declamations by the boys, and also singing, were another special feature of school life designed to foster confidence and a sense of occasion. But on the whole music played no very great part at Clermont, and certainly not in Francis' own life. It always remained no more than an adjunct for him and a means for the worthier celebration of the liturgy. We are told, however, that he had a good voice and an accurate ear.

As the student progressed up the school—by examination only, strict justice being done, and the masters specially instructed not to yield to pressure on the part of importunate parents—the *praelectio* assumed greater significance than ever and filled more of the teaching time. In rhetoric this was reduced to four hours daily of which one was Greek. In philosophy the *praelectio* became a lecture pure and simply. The students' contribution by essay and declamation, on a larger and more adult scale, became increasingly important as compared with learning which was now done out of class and alone. By this time a boy was expected to be able to speak, impromptu if necessary, on any set topic, and to show that he had mastered the techniques of rhetoric as set out by Aristotle. These techniques, as anyone who glances at this now for all practical purposes neglected treatise can see, included the knowledge of a great deal of psychology. It was no use trying to convince, sway or move a visible or invisible audience by your words if you did not know how the human mind works and responds, your own mind to begin with, and then that of others. Francis de Sales' preaching and his *Introduction to the Devout Life* presuppose a thorough study of the art of persuasion.

The teachers in a large college such as Clermont were well aware that they lacked, to some extent, personal contact with individual pupils. In order to achieve this they had to select, and this they did in the fairest way possible by forming a self-perpetuating spiritual and intellectual commando group known as the sodality. Its constitution was part of the *Ratio Studiorum* as it was a vital part of the whole educative process. This congregation, approved by the pope in 1580 under the title and patronage of the Blessed Virgin of the Assumption, recruited members by selection from among boys who took both their religion and their work seriously. It had the double function of being a devotional confraternity and a literary academy, with separate branches for each of the main school classes. Soon after he entered Clermont, Francis was considered distinguished enough to be admitted to the sodality, and was in due course elected secretary and later president, that is, the leader of the group under a moderator appointed from among the professors. This election was by a secret vote of the members; the president had to be someone who "excelled in virtue, talent and learning"[14] and who stood out clearly among his fellows. While the spiritual part consisted for the main in a special service once a week, and in the promise to frequent the sacraments at least once a month, the group met as an academy on Sundays when papers or poems were read by members, or a debate took place, in Latin, of course. "Enigmas, inscriptions and symbolical devices," that is, emblems were composed and lettered or designed and submitted for general criticism. In this way the emblematic habit of mind, without which Francis' writing is unthinkable, was fostered. Once or twice a year on a feast day of Our Lady there was an open day at Clermont and work was exhibited. Sometimes the moderator himself read a paper on some literary topic, but this was rare. Each individual member was urged to use his own initiative, develop his inventive powers, and do some personal literary work according to his own bent of mind. It is not necessary to stress the literary value of such personal training and experience over a whole school career.

Without exception, the saint's biographers, ancient and modern, have only mentioned the sodality as a spiritual stamping ground, but the intellectual and literary side is surely of great significance too. Later on, this former president of the sodality founded his own literary academy, the Académie Florimontane, established in 1606 with the help of his friend, the senator and later president of the Chambéry parliament, Antoine Favre. He too was an old boy of Clermont, having preceded Francis by ten years. Favre's daughter was one of the first Visitation sisters; his son Claude Favre de Vaugelas, the author of *Remarques sur la langue française* (1647). In founding their academy the two friends were continuing a tradition well known to them both from their Clermont days and which had reached France through Italian humanist influence in school and court.

Monsieur de Boisy did not intend that his son's seven or eight years in Paris should be spent entirely over books and in the classroom. They were meant to be important formative years in his career as a courtier and nobleman. He had to learn to present himself suitably in the great houses where the De Sales family had connections, and also at the court itself. *Civileté*, or the art of producing oneself courteously in public, was not left to chance any more than was oratory; nor was it a mere set of exterior conventions followed in a craven spirit of social conformity. It was a training which affected the whole man, and the accomplishments connected with *civileté* were merely the outward expression of a fundamental attitude towards society, slowly formed and perfected from boyhood in a man of good standing. Monsieur Déage was in charge of the social arrangements and had to see that his pupil learnt fencing, riding and dancing. A similar sort of mystique was attached to these accomplishments as was in a later age transferred to games in the public school ethos. They did, of course, also serve as exercise, by no means neglected by humanist educators, well versed in the Greek attitude to physical culture.

We are told by his nephew that Francis considered these exercises rather useless for the kind of life he was planning for himself in secret, but that he obediently did what was required.

As he is said to have distinguished himself in these skills, his assent was perhaps more than merely formal. They certainly left their mark on the whole man: he was noted for both outer and inner poise. He also learnt the more advanced techniques of horsemanship. Equitation took place in one of the great indoor riding academies, the idea of the *manège* having been brought to Paris from Italy in the course of that century. For fencing he went to a private master. The sword he wore until the day he put on his clerical robe was not just a decorative symbol. He learnt to fight in real earnest, and when occasion warranted, as happened one night in a melée in Padua, he was easily able to disarm his adversaries.

Some knowledge of the formal dances of the time was necessary for his entrée to houses like that of the Duke of Mercoeur where his father had been a page earlier in the century. On festive occasions he had to be able to take his place in the formal, measured dances of the day, the gavotte and the minuet, which actually originated in France at about this time though we are apt to associate both with a later rococo age.[15] There was also the more dashing courante brought from the courts of Renaissance Italy. Again, skill in dancing of this kind was more than a mere badge of social distinction, for the ability to manage formal, intricate patterns of disciplined movement was an artistic skill fostering grace and a sense of rhythm in other spheres. Again, there is no mention of any training in music as such.

He was not, however, unaware of the potential dangers of dancing, nor can one suppose him to have been blind to the licentiousness of student and social life in the Paris of this time, and especially at court. We are told that he made purity the subject of continual prayer and strengthened his will-power by making a formal vow of chastity in the church next to the college, Saint-Étienne-des-Grès. He had the habit of praying there by an ancient statue of Our Lady, Notre Dame de la Bonne Déliverance, also called Notre Dame des Âmes en peine. It was to her help that he looked in his struggle to keep himself intact. The profound insight that he later showed in his description of emotional attitudes between the sexes shows that he knew from observation and psychological awareness what he was talking about. His advice on this subject in the *Introduction* is penetrating and still relevant.

His longing for intactness in this sphere, his precocious understanding in the years of adolescent turmoil of what freely chosen virginity for a religious motive really meant, is stressed, though in rather different terms, by all the early biographers. One of the most vivid details is that related by Charles-Auguste de Sales[16] who reports how Francis used to make his way to the Louvre and enter the state apartments, as he was entitled to do, to watch the Queen of Henri III at her meal. He always tried to get close to her and touch the hem of her garment, for he felt that virtue went out from her. She was distinguished for her marital faithfulness and purity under shockingly difficult conditions. With other people, too, who were distinguished for chastity in a licentious age, Francis would make the same instinctive attempt to keep in actual physical touch with the virtue so deeply preoccupying him.

This preoccupation was a natural part of his development but which in a gifted and emotional boy, living away from a normal home and family background, can easily produce a state of extreme nervous tension. The general excitement at this stage tends to find a focus in whatever aspect of experience presents the greatest value, and for Francis this was his own personal religion, his attitude to God. The devil, says the saint's first biographer, Dom Jean de Saint François, considered Francis to be doing so well that a challenge was indicated; God allowed His servant to suffer a violent assault so as to prepare "this great master of spiritual fencing" for his future combat on God's side. In Paris the powers of darkness fought against God for the possession of this young Job's soul, and the points of attack selected by the adversary were the emotions and the intellect.[17] To make things worse, the encounter took place at the psychologically difficult time of mid-winter when resistance is in any case at its lowest ebb and when a physical illness seemed to be threatening Francis.

The crisis came in December 1586 and the first two weeks of the following January. Francis was nineteen and well launched in his philosophy class which brought so much new scientific material to bear on his consciousness: the nature of matter, the mathematics of space and time, the creative process at work behind the structure of living organisms. At the same time Monsieur Déage was now taking him to the Sorbonne for certain lecture courses in theology. One of the great subjects of debate at the faculty at this time was that of predestination, the problem posed by Calvin, who took the extreme position, as it seemed to the opposite camp, of defending it outright. Christian humanists, Erasmus, and later on, the Jesuit Molina, opposed it out and out, while the official opinion of the Church, represented by St. Augustine and St. Thomas Aquinas, took up what appeared as an intermediate and therefore inconclusive position. God predestined His saints to glory independently of their good works, which He indeed foresaw and for which He gave them grace, but this was only a general part of His original will for them and thus a manifestation of His justice.

Predestination expressed in human terms did not present itself to Francis as an intellectual conundrum so closely connected with the nature of God in Himself as to be in the last resort insoluble for the finite mind. He never seems to have been in any serious doubt, intellectually, about his position; the problem was an emotional, psychological one, and very probably mystical as well. Unlike most of the people around him who argued the matter as a theological abstraction, Francis saw it as a burning life question: "Am I myself, tempted as I am by the pleasures I see going on all around me, and inclined to evil as I know myself to be, am I fated to be damned or to be saved? Am I destined to be parted from God for ever and ever, and shall I perhaps never be able to show Him my love, however hard I try here and now to live the good life?" At a time of intense emotional stress, he opted for the answer of despair, and no amount of rational argument, no effort of his own or of his teachers and friends could reach him. To a person of less vivid faith and love, the question could never have become so real. Had he really been evil, he would not have hesitated to choose the easy way out. But it was part of his problem that he could not see his own quandary in the light of logic. For weeks on end he wept and cried aloud to God, mourning the loss of Him and of all he had ever lived and worked for. Sleepless, he knelt by his bed in tears: "O Love, O

Beauty, am I never to know You, to take my joy in You? O Mary, my mother, am I never to see you in your Son's kingdom? Did not my beloved Jesus die for me too and redeem me?"[18]

His state rapidly deteriorated; he was caught up in a tangle of emotional argument which expressed itself in an intense depression. According to his biographers, his melancholy forced its way out and appeared as an allover yellowing of his skin which was, as a rule, healthy but now looked like wax; he suffered a catastrophic loss of weight and such severe attacks of pain that he could neither sleep, eat, nor drink. He dragged himself around more dead than alive but refused to take to his bed.[19] From these symptoms one would be inclined to think that his despair came upon him at the same time as an actual illness and that the mental state was aggravated by the physical. This is in no way to question or decry the spiritual validity of an experience that bears many signs of a mystical trial in a personality as sane and confident as Francis had always shown himself to be. There is no reason why a physical illness should not form part of a perhaps mystical crisis which may well affect the whole man. Indeed, St. John of the Cross implies that this is not unusual.[20] The fact remains that the details given by contemporary witnesses correspond, as far as one can judge, to an attack of jaundice caused, perhaps, by some gallstone disorder which is known to have an intensely depressing effect.[21] The evidence rests on the account of his servant, on the witness of Monsieur Déage and of two fellow students. There was also Francis' own account to Madame de Chantal, as well as some written evidence preserved through the canonization documents.

One could wish there were some letters in which Francis had expressed his feelings, but with the exception of one insignificant thank-you letter, the whole correspondence of the Paris years was burnt when the castle at Thorens was looted and burnt in 1634. In any cast it is very unlikely that he would have written the kind of personal letter one might now expect. All we have is a brief *protestation* and a page of quotations from the Psalms, both copied from what he had himself written down at the time. These Scripture verses which he used to say and sob out aloud as he knelt by his bed at night may seem impersonal, but to one who knew the whole psalter off by heart and whose prayer was naturally cast in liturgical forms, David's timeless cry for help was the most natural and powerful way to express what lay far beyond the reach of his own words:

> Will God then leave me forsaken forever, and in anger forget to show me mercy? Let God arise, and His enemies will vanish before Him like smoke, and as wax melts in the fire, the devil's assaults will perish. God is our refuge and our strength; we will not fear even if the earth should fall to pieces all around us and the hills be carried away into the depths of the sea. My enemies have prepared a snare for my feet, they bowed down my soul, they dug a pit in my path. I will take refuge under the shelter of Thy wings till the storm passes by; I will cry out to the most high God, He will snatch my soul from the lion's den. God save me! See how the waters close about me shoulder high! I am like one who sticks fast in deep mire, with no ground under his feet, one who has ventured out to mid-ocean to be drowned by the tempest. Save me from sinking in the mire, rescue me from my enemies, from the deep waters that surround me; let me not sink beneath the flood, swallowed up in its depths, let not the well's mouth close over me! Shall not my soul be subject to God? For from Him is my salvation. In Thee, Lord, have I hoped; let me not be confounded.[22]

The prayers begin and end on a strong note of hope which is never absent throughout the earthquake and storm which have engulfed him, with the waters closing, as it were, over his head, and his feet seeming to sink ever deeper into quicksand. He saw himself, too, as ensnared by his enemy, as having stumbled into a trap and being exposed to wild beasts who threatened to tear him to pieces. No words of his own could have described his state of inner disintegration more vividly than the series of symbols he took from the Bible, and it is worth noticing that he who was to build so much of his own work on a theory of the spiritual effectiveness of images, instinctively chose passages which gave him a concrete and tangible picture of his plight.

His greatest fear, as he told Madame de Chantal, was that if he were indeed damned, as it seemed to him, he would never in all eternity be able to show his love for God and for Mary.[23] As the weeks passed he clung firmly to the resolution that he would at least show his love by serving God all the more faithfully here on earth, and he would accept his own damnation because God had apparently willed it. All that really mattered was that God's decrees should be fulfilled. Put like this, the proposition sounds so tragically senseless to a Christian who believes in a loving God that it is hard to imagine how Francis could have held it. Yet it is obvious from his *protestation*[24] that this was his line of thought. "If I am damned because I deserve it, that is, on my own merits, at least let me not be among those who curse your holy name," was his final word on the subject and at the same the clearest possible demonstration of his true love of God. He had driven his ideas to an extreme point of pseudo-logical absurdity which corresponded somehow to the extreme state of nervous tension in which he found himself. He had reached a point of heroic acceptance, giving himself up unconditionally to God and being subject to Him, without any reliance on his own very considerable merits, his own young strength into which, without knowing it, he had put much of his trust in the course of his struggle for virtue. He was to learn the mystic's first and last lesson—to rely on God alone. And now he was prepared, as far as in him lay, for the ending of his trial which came from above. As yet, his feelings, so deeply disturbed over the past weeks, lagged behind the reasoned conclusion which he had so far not been able to accept as yet on the emotional level, making it possible for head and heart to come together again in a conflict healed.

Walking home one day from the Louvre—his physical condition must already have been somewhat improved by then as this is a good half-hour's walk along the Seine—he crossed the bridge by Notre Dame and went up the hill just past his college, where he turned into a side road to enter Saint-Étienne-des-Grès. In a small chapel to the left of the high altar there stood the ancient statue, so well known to him, of Notre Dame des Âmes en peine, as she was called by those who came to her in distress. He knelt down, picked up the little wooden tablet on which was pasted a handwritten copy of St. Bernard's prayer to Our Lady, the Memorare, and said it right through in a spirit of deep and childlike trust. When he rose up to go, he suddenly felt "as if his torment had fallen about his feet like a leper's scales"[25] and he realized that from this moment he was completely cured. The leprosy of temptation and despair which had made of him an outcast and put him, as he thought, beyond the reach of God's love and robbed him of his own capacity to love God, vanished in an instant as he knelt before the Virgin Mother and her Child.

She holds a sceptre, the sign of her royal power; the Child on her arm reaches out towards her with one hand while in the other He holds an orb surmounted by a cross—the world redeemed. Madonna and Child are shown inclined towards one another, their faces serene and simple, with the half smile so characteristic of medieval French sculpture of this kind. The Virgin's painted red robe with its full blue mantle is draped in a way that gives the stone fabric a sense of life and movement while the line of the folds leads the eye naturally to the arm and hand which form, as it were, a throne for the Child King. Both figures are now crowned, but this is a twentieth-century addition. The medieval statue had no need to state so overtly the symbols of kingship, perhaps because the royal power in heaven was far more present to people's consciousness then and needed no stressing. The statue is not a great work of art, the Virgin's broad, placid face has an almost archaic simplicity, but the indefinable look of tenderness and understanding in the Madonna's calm gaze remains in the mind of those who come to worship the King as a child in her arms.

Like others of her kind at Chartres, Rocamadour and in Francis' own Savoy, this "Vierge Noire" had been in her shrine from time immemorial. The nearly life-size black stone figure of the early fourteenth century had replaced a wooden one, blackened with age, which in its turn had perhaps been adapted from a Mother Earth image of pagan times. As in the case of many of the ancient black Madonnas, its appeal of motherliness was to something very deep in the human consciousness. The statue was the concrete focus of a large local confraternity which must have been well known to Francis as it was confirmed by Pope Gregory XIII in 1585 and enriched with further indulgences.

The members pledged themselves in a special way to help their brethren when they were ill or distressed, and they gave alms for the redemption of prisoners who were locked up for debt.

Twice a year, in spring and summer, the statue was carried in procession down to the Seine and across the bridge to Notre Dame, the mother church on which Saint Étienne depended. After the return of the procession, which was always a colorful event for the rue Saint Jacques, the officers of the confraternity, and anyone else who liked to join them went to the prison to free debtors with the money that had been collected. The debtors were, as a rule, simple tradesmen of the district, locksmiths, carpenters, bakers, whose gratitude to Our Lady through whom charity had been mobilized in this practical way knew no bounds. Her little chapel was rarely deserted at any time of the day, and this Madonna was known not only all over Paris but in the surrounding country as well. Even the court held it in high favor which increased still more in the course of the next century.[26]

It was no mere chance, then, that brought Francis to pray before her at such a crisis in his life. When the solution had been prepared by his unconditional surrender, not to despair, but to God, Notre Dame de la Délivrance was the channel for the grace which ended the conflict. This was, as far as is known, his only great spiritual trial. It helped to confirm the confident, optimistic attitude that was natural to him, looking on God, as St. Chantal said, as a beloved child looks to its father. It also helped him to a store of personal insight into one of the fundamental and often misunderstood tenets of the Calvinists in his future diocese. On the rational level he had studied the problem of predestination from every angle, and he continued to do this afterwards, without any fear of falling back into his despair, a proof that the difficulty had been far more than a merely intellectual one.

Looking back on his experience four years later in Padua when he was writing out lecture notes about the reprobation of the wicked, he added a personal summary of his own position of confidence: "The light is too dazzling for my blind eyes, and I am prepared to be ignorant of everything else for the sake of the Father's own knowledge which is—Christ crucified." In describing his attitude he seems to hear God addressing him directly in words analogous to those of the Scriptures: "'Have no fear, My son, I do not seek the death of a sinner but rather that he should live to serve Me and grow in holiness. Your sickness is not unto death; so take heart, My little servant [*serve parve*], unworthy you may be, but you are faithful, hoping in Me, willing as you were to glorify My name by your damnation, had this been My will. I will establish you over much and you shall praise My name where bliss is eternal.' Then I will reply as I did before: 'Amen, Father, because this has seemed good to You, Amen, Jesus, Mary.'"[27]

"I learnt many things in Paris to please my father," Francis was to say later, "and a few to please myself." Monsieur Déage was at times rather worried about the intensity of his pupil's religious feelings, his confirmed habit of solitary walks and his apparent indifference to worldly advantages. He was beginning to be afraid Francis might enter some religious order before he could ever get him back to Savoy. As for the particular direction his thoughts might be taking, for a president of the sodality and a boy who regularly made the *Spiritual Exercises* of St. Ignatius in the modified form then customary at Clermont, the Company itself might have been indicated. But the first rule of the retreat giver was to leave the soul alone with God and to be strenuously on guard not to exert influence.[28] There were also the Capuchin Franciscans whose monastery near the Louvre Francis was known to frequent almost daily, especially towards the end of his Paris stay when the twenty-four-year-old widower, Duke Henri de Joyeuse, a member of his own Lorraine court circle, entered there as Frère Ange. Francis liked to watch him serving Mass clothed in his poor coarse habit, barefooted, humble, where a short while before he had seen him at court resplendent in all his finery. "What an example for us. God wants to tell us something by this, He wants to call us," he was heard to say.

In his way Francis profited by such calls. It is known that on three days of the week during this last year after his recovery he fasted and wore a hairshirt.[29] This must have been done with the permission of his director in the sodality. He went to Mass every day and to the sacraments week by week, and he began each day with a period of prayer: "From that time he meditated diligently on divine things and gave himself up to interior recollection, always remembering the presence of God. Now that his heart was on flame with love, he lifted it up continually towards that uncreated beauty which was gradually being revealed to his soul."[30] As the symbol of his complete giving up of self he had renewed his vow of virginity before Notre Dame de la Délivrance and had at the same time promised, in thanksgiving for his healing, to say the rosary every day. He kept his promise to the end, referring to it in later years as his "spell of duty at the Queen's court."

According to the account of his biographers and the testimony of his friends, he was greatly beloved in Paris among the students and teachers and also beyond the college in his own particular circle. There was grief when the time came for him to go in the early summer of 1588 after the final examinations in the arts faculty which took place just before Easter. When he and his escort consisting of Monsieur Déage and the two servants rode out of Paris, four of Francis' friends attached themselves to his group and traveled with him as far as Lyons. There Francis was met by a Savoyard friend of his father's who came with horses from the stables at home. "I found him so attractive and impressive, his whole bearing had such beauty that I thought most highly of him ever afterwards," said this same friend in his testimony.[31]

What was he like in his twenty-first year? The witnesses are too unanimous in attributing great personal attractiveness to him for this to have been mere exaggeration. In his Padua notebook he copied from his reading the observation that virtue does not only render man beautiful within but also affects his outward appearance.[32] Over the years Francis had developed the beauty of expression which comes from within. The sense of rightness and harmony about him was so strong that even strangers would stop to look at him as he passed them in the street. He had a certain easy and unselfconscious dignity in his bearing, was a little above average height, well built and always carefully dressed. Nothing in his clothes betrayed the hair shirt beneath. One must think of him in the becoming costume of the late Renaissance, something like a character out of one of Shakespeare's Italian comedies: a frilled collar framed his rather long, oval face, he wore a wide-shouldered doublet or short jacket shaped in to the waist, long trunk hose with puffed breeches whose full pleats were lined with a lighter colored satin. A short cloak hung from his shoulders, his sword at his left side was attached to an embroidered belt. On his head he wore a softly draped velvet cap with a curling plume. A small tuft of feathers, a panache, also decorated the other type of fashionable headgear in the 1580s, a close fitting rimless toque. The hat was an important status symbol and a man of rank was entitled to keep it on even in church, a privilege of which Francis, it is said, never availed himself. He had the habit, even in his student days, of lifting his hat when he passed the outside of a church. He was known in later years for his practice of doffing his hat to his inferiors in rank and even to his own clerical staff.

When he arrived at his uncle's castle at Brens in the Chablais plain where his parents were still living at that time, the whole household, his parents, his uncle and aunt, brothers, sisters, cousins and servants "all ran out with great joy to meet him as he came in sight. His mother embraced and kissed him with tears, his father was delighted beyond all telling to find him so capable and accomplished. Both of them could have gone on listening all day and all night while he talked and his words flowed more sweetly than honey. He now had plenty of time to see his friends and relations, and wherever he went people marveled at him and loved him." [33]

NOTES

1. Antoine Dufournet, *La jeunesse de Saint François de Sales, 1567-1602* (Paris, 1942), 26, and *Oeuvres*, 22:xiv. The date 1578 for the actual beginning of the saint's education, suggested by E.-J. Lajeunie, O.P., *Saint François de Sales: l'homme, la pensée, l'action,* 2 vols. (Paris, 1966), 1:121-22, seems to me to be too early and is based on negative evidence only. The date of Francis' return from Paris, 1588, is undisputed, and if he really left Savoy in 1578, this would have meant a ten-year absence from home. Also, the confidence and independence shown by Francis on the day of his arrival in Paris would seem to be more in keeping with an adolescent boy of thirteen or fourteen than with a child of barely eleven, even allowing for an earlier age of maturity in the sixteenth century.

2. Charles-Auguste de Sales, *Histoire du bien-heureux François de Sales,* 2 vols. (1634; Paris, 1857), 1:10 (hereafter Charles-Auguste).

3. Dom Jean de Saint François, *La vie du bien-heureux Messire François de Sales* (Paris, 1624), 30 (hereafter Dom Jean).

4. Charles-Auguste, 1:9.

5. From the Latin text of 5 September 1591, *Oeuvres*, 22:84-85.

6. Founded in 1530. Among the professors at the Collège Royal (later Collège de France) were: Génébrard, the scholar who applied philological and historical principles to the study of the Scriptures; Ramus (1515-1572), grammarian and philosopher and a precursor of Descartes; Amyot (1513-1593), one of the renewers of language by his translation of Plutarch; Passerat, one of the authors of the *Satire Ménippée*; Dorat, the grandfather of Jean Goulu whose name in religion was Dom Jean de Saint François, General of the Feuillant Order and one of the first biographers of St. Francis de Sales.

7. Allan Farrell, S.J., *The Jesuit Code of Liberal Education* (Milwaukee, 1938), 219.

8. *Monumenta Pedagogica Societatis Jesu* quae primam rationem studiorum anno 1586 editam praecessere (Madrid, 1901), in the series *Monumenta Historica Societatis Jesu* (*MHSJ*). Lajeunie says that the courses at Clermont can be no more than a matter of conjecture (1:126). These contemporary Jesuit documents do, however, give us facts which go beyond speculation.

9. W. H. Woodward, *Studies in Education during the Age of the Renaissance* (Cambridge, 1924), 14.

10. Farrell, 49, 11.

11. For the philosophy curriculum, see *Monumenta Pedagogica*, 485-515 (secs. 40-46).

12. See W. T. Costello, S.J., *The Scholastic Curriculum at Early Seventeenth-Century Cambridge* (Cambridge, Massachusetts, 1958). The late Fr. Costello of Harvard was a Fulbright research scholar at Emmanuel College, Cambridge, from 1949-1950. His book is a mine of valuable firsthand information from manuscript sources.

13. For bibliography, see Edna Purdie's article on Jesuit Drama in the *Oxford Companion to the Theatre*, 2nd ed. (London, 1957).

14. Farrell, 322.

15. J. Tabouret, *Orchéographie* (Paris, 1598).

16. Charles-Auguste, 1:16.

17. Dom Jean, 34. It seems right to follow, in the main, the interpretation placed on the Paris crisis by the saint's best biographer, a trained theologian who was, moreover, an expert in mystical theology. See "The First Biography (1624)," in the present volume.

18. *Oeuvres*, 22:18.

19. Charles-Auguste, 1:14, and Dom Jean, 36.

20. *The Dark Night of the Soul*, Bk. 2, ch. 6 onwards, in *The Works of St. John of the Cross*, translated by E. Allison Peers (London, 1934), 1:409ff.

21. Although he was rather young at nineteen for a gallstone attack, his later medical history is that of a chronic gallbladder sufferer and the anatomy made immediately after his death in 1622 confirmed this. The organ was found to be crammed full of stones of every color, a feature which greatly impressed his contemporaries and was illustrated in an emblem book as proving the violence the saint had to do to himself to subdue his naturally quick temper and inclination to anger. Exactly the same phenomenon had come to light in the anatomy of St. Ignatius of Loyola.

22. *Oeuvres*, 22:14-18. I have kept the sequence of these quotations while omitting some of them. They are taken from Psalms 76, 67, 45, 56, 68, 61 and 30 (Knox and Douay version). Slight variations from the traditional text of the Vulgate will be observed. They are Francis' own adaptations. It is interesting that in describing the dark night in the passages already noted, St. John of the Cross selects some of the same images from the Psalmist, notably that of the flood, tempest and mire. This work, though written ca. 1578, was not published till 1619. Although St. Francis never actually quotes the Carmelite mystic, Pierre Serouet, O.C.D., *De la vie dévote à la vie mystique: Sainte Thérèse d'Avila, Saint François de Sales*, Études Carmélitaines (Bruges, 1958), 382ff, thinks it not at all unlikely that he did know him, as some of his works circulated in manuscript copies in France long before they were printed. Serouet (125ff) thinks that the Paris crisis was definitely a mystical and not only a moral one; in St. John's terms, it was probably a particularly painful form of the night of the senses. See the illuminating summary of the various views of this crisis by William Gallagher, O.S.F.S., "The State of Salesian Studies," *Salesian Studies*, 1, no. 1 (March 1962): 14-15.

23. *St. Francis de Sales: A Testimony by St. Chantal*, newly edited in translation with an introduction by Elisabeth Stopp (London/ Hyattsville, 1967), 45 (hereafter *Testimony*).

24. See *Oeuvres*, 22:19-20, for the Latin text.

25. *Testimony*, 45.

26. The *Vierge Noire* survived the turmoils of the Revolution. It was hidden by a lady who escaped the guillotine and in thanksgiving bestowed the statue on the Sisters of St. Thomas of Villanova, whose motherhouse in now in the Paris suburb of Neuilly-sur-Seine. The statue is still a center of pilgrimage. It stands in a nineteenth-century setting not unworthy of it, if only by a striking contrast, and by the excellence of lighting. Several books have been written on the statue of which the latest, containing a full history, is Marie-Andre, *La Vierge Noire de Paris: Châtelaine de Neuilly N.D. de Bonne Délivrance* (Paris, 1958).

27. *Oeuvres*, 22:64-67. The text is in Latin.

28. *The Spiritual Exercises of Saint Ignatius*, translated by Thomas Corbishley, S.J., (London, 1963), 16 (par. 15).

29. Testimony of his schoolfriend, François Thabuis, in *Saint François de Sales par les témoins de sa vie: Textes extraits des procès de béatification*, edited by Roger Devos (Annecy, 1967), 53.

30. Dom Jean, 34.

31. Testimony of Nicolas de Couz, *First Process*, 3:595.

32. *Oeuvres*, 22:34.

33. Charles-Auguste, 1:16. As Brens lies in a hollow, the Lake of Geneva is hidden from view by a low-lying hill. A substantial part of the original building, still inhabited, remains. It is surrounded by a wide moat and the drawbridge now forms a permanent entry leading to a massive portal dating from the saint's time. Within it are hidden seats for guards. The position of the castle made it vulnerable to attack and it was evidently heavily fortified. Behind the portal lies the now open courtyard with a number of huge, ancient chestnuts. The church in the village close by has been carefully restored and still contains the burial vaults of the De Sales family.

II

MEDITATIONS ON THE CHURCH (1595-96)

Francis de Sales first mentioned this work toward the end of January 1595, in a letter to Antoine Favre. The date that he puts at the end of his dedicatory letter to the Gentlemen of Thonon is that of January 25, "Jour de la Conversion de saint Pol," a feast that sets the tone for the whole work to follow, and that in our own day is widely known throughout all the churches of Christendom as the final day of the Unity Octave. The *Meditations on the Church (Méditations sur l'Église)* were, insofar as this was possible in Francis' day, a genuine attempt at a dialogue, at a true conversation on points of difference. In any case the book deserves better than the title under which it has come to be known: *The Controversies (Les Controverses)*. It was given this name in analogy to Robert Bellarmine's *De Controversiis Christianae Fidei* (1586-93), which Francis used as a reference book in the composition of his own work, and the title was meant to confer status on a piece of newly discovered evidence for the saint's second canonization process. In 1655 his nephew found the manuscript in a box cemented into a hiding hole in the archive room of the castle of La Thuile. Without any record having been made of what had been done, the case had been walled up at some earlier stage for greater safety against plundering French soldiers, who had, in fact, destroyed many family letters at Sales. The work consisted of some 275 folio sheets mostly in Francis' own writing, a rough copy, in the main, untitled and with incomplete headings within the text. It was copied into the canonization volumes and then prepared and edited as *Les Controverses* in 1672 as the eighth and last volume of his complete works.[1] Dom Benedict Mackey, the editor of the Annecy *Oeuvres*, and himself the translator of the work under the title *The Catholic Controversy* (1886), kept the same designation for his new and greatly improved text of 1892.

This title, which was quite appropriate according to the ideas of an earlier century, finds little appeal in our own; but, what is far more significant, it was one consciously avoided by the author himself, who referred to his work as "my meditations on the Church." He also called it his *Mémorial*, a word he frequently used for occasional writings and which can best be rendered as "a summary of points," an informal communication. "De haereticorum hujus temporis instabilitate meditationes animo volvam" he writes to Favre in January 1595.[2] On another occasion he speaks of his "opusculum," or "little work." He was very sensitive to the impact of words and to exact shades of meaning. To a friend who wanted to use the phrase "insuffance de l'Écriture" in an argument in Geneva, he wrote that the term "insuffance" would make his hearers cry out in contradiction. "I would prefer to admit that the Scriptures are wholly sufficient for our instruction but that the insufficiency lies in our own selves; for without the tradition and teaching of the Church we don't understand how to get at the meaning of the Scriptures."[3] It comes to much the same thing, one may say; it is just a question of emphasis. But for a craftsman in words, as Francis de Sales already was at that stage, the precise connotation and emotional resonance of words was so important that the title, which sets the atmosphere of the whole work, should surely accord with the author's intention rather than with that of his editors. And what the author wanted was a personal and informal approach. Had the *Meditations* been published when they were written, that is, between January 1595, and the summer of the following year, they would have been the first attempt at an informal work of theology in the French language. One critic goes as far as to say that, though less distinguished as a literary work, the *Meditations* would have had the same liberating impact on theological writing in *1595* as Montaigne's *Essays* had on philosophy and the study of man.[4]

The work reflects the circumstances in which it was written, that is, not as a book intended for publication after it was finished, but as a number of communications that appeared in serialized form. It is clear, however, that Francis had a coherent plan of work before he ever put pen to paper. By a series of progressive reflections he wanted to build up a true picture of the Church in order to prove that its claims were justified; each separate point, or "article" as he called it, was designed to stand on its own while supplementing what had gone before and pointing ahead to the further argument envisaged. As the articles were finished he had them copied, possibly even printed, though this has never been proved, and delivered by hand to the "gentlemen of Thonon," that is, the Calvinist elders to whom his dedicatory letter is addressed. They were all men he knew personally and whom he passed in the streets of the town day by day; one of them was a cousin of his.

A series of informal meditations, however, even when they follow a plan, do not necessarily make a book, only the raw material for one. In a letter about his literary plans written fourteen years later Francis said:

> I have some material by me which might help begin-
> ners in the art of evangelical preaching; and I would
> like to complete this with practical instructions on how
> to convert heretics by sermons. I want to describe a
> method of disproving all the most notorious arguments
> of our adversaries, making use of a style which instructs
> but also moves, at the same time disarming heretics and
> comforting Catholics. For this book I want to use a
> number of meditations I wrote during my five years in
> the Chablais where I preached with no other books
> except the Bible and the works of the great Bellarmine.[5]

On Francis de Sales' own showing, then, the *Meditations* should not be seen as a rounded-off work complete with a technical title but as a careful first draft, as the informal exploration of a topic, that of the idea of the Church. Moreover, the author did not finish the last part of his work, which, according to his own clearly formulated design, was to have been important. Editors and biographers have not sufficiently stressed the true nature of this work, its incompleteness, the atmosphere of improvisation which lies about it, the very considerable textual problems connected with the manuscript. The Annecy editor and his Dominican brother, Peter Paul Mackey, who was working in Rome at the time on the Leonine edition of St. Thomas Aquinas, made a transcription of the difficult and wrongly ordered manuscript in Rome, at the Chigi Library, and then completed it with some sheets newly discovered at Annecy. The order thought to have been intended by Francis de Sales was restored, headings were supplied where missing, variant readings were introduced in footnotes but also within the body of the text where the editors considered this indicated.[6] In fact, the editors have done their work so efficiently that anyone picking up the first volume of the Annecy edition which contains the *Meditations* would quite naturally assume this to be a work on a level with the saint's finished literary productions, for instance, the *Introduction*. The corrective to this is to realize that Francis de Sales did not even mention the *Meditations* in the list of his works that he himself gave in his preface to the *Treatise on the Love of God* in 1616, whereas he included not only the *Defense of the Standard of the Holy Cross*, also written during his missionary years, but even a *Meditation on the Creed* of some dozen pages.[7]

Bearing in mind, then, the true nature of the *Meditations on the Church*, one can now approach the text, and the best way to get a grasp of its structure, not immediately obvious from the detailed Table of Contents,[8] is to consider Francis de Sales' own introductions. He wrote three of these, one for each part of the work; he drafted them carefully, making many minute alterations, improving the rhythm, order, and disposition, clarifying the meaning, softening the edges of any statement that may have seemed harsh. One has the impression that he wrote these opening pages when he was planning his work, and as an aid to its more detailed structure. At any rate the general design of the work emerges from them as a simple, clear, bold, and, in the light of the times, a wholly original plan. In the first part he shows what signs distinguish the true Church, in the second he describes the rules of faith by which the Church lives, in the third he proposes to demonstrate the working out of these rules in practice. These parts have three, eight, and two chapters respectively, which are in turn divided into articles, eighty-one in all: twenty-eight in the first part, forty in the second, and thirteen in the last unfinished section. The work as it stands centers, therefore, on the second part, which bears the main exposition of the matter introduced in the first part and worked out in a practical way in the last section. The clarity of this scheme is in itself greatly satisfying; one has that sense of order produced out of chaos which is the mark of a well composed literary work, the more so as the structure nowhere obtrudes itself but emerges naturally with the progress of ideas.

In his short letter of dedication, Francis gives the clue to the atmosphere that pervades his work: it is that of the spoken word for which it is a mere substitute. In some instances he was simply writing out the substance of sermons that he had already given but which the Calvinists refused to attend; for he would have liked his friends to hear living words that have a "secret vigor" whereas on paper they seem to die. Writing, on the other hand, is a greater test of the quality of the content than is speech, and it can also be pondered at leisure. Appealing to their sense of fair play, he begs them to hear his description of the Church, now that for so many years they have only been able to listen to the negative side. The introduction to the first part then states the theme he proposes to treat: the greatest scandal in the world is the present disunity among Christians; the obstacle to unity is that the Church is itself a scandal to those who have separated themselves from her. He therefore wants to show that this Susanna stands wrongly accused, both for general reasons applicable to all heretical attacks, and in particular instances, familiar to all Swiss local Calvinists. He proposes to describe the Church. That is, of course, what every apologist tries to do, but not directly, "in a straight line": "I will try to make every line of my discourse converge on this one single point as on its center,"[9] not trying to say anything new, for that would hardly be possible, but saying it in a new aspect. In this way he stresses the great importance he assigns to the order and method of his statement and this is where its originality lies: "The garment is old, all that's mine is the needle and thread, and all I have had to do is to unpick the old and sew it up again in my own way."[10] He hopes that the work, humble though it is, will find a way to their heart as something homely and indigenous, written only for them by a fellow countryman: "The look of it is altogether Savoyard, and one of the most wholesome and ultimate remedies is a return to one's native air . . . I will begin in God's name then, humbly begging Him to let His words flow very gently and like fresh dew into your hearts."[11]

In the opening chapter of his description of the Church and at the very foundation of the whole work, he puts the idea of the Church's divine mission from God through Jesus Christ, a mission which the ministers have not received; the Church is and always has been a visible society whose authority is now being violated by self-appointed men. At the very start, then, Francis de Sales insinuates himself between people and pastors, making his initial description of the true nature of the Church implicitly serve the end of showing up false claims. This is his emphasis throughout and this is what distinguishes his work immediately from controversy and polemics of the usual kind: he consistently uses defense as a method of attack, not because he is incapable of taking the offensive, as is perfectly clear throughout, but because he believes that this is the only right way to wage religious warfare. In two further chapters, which are, perhaps, the most impressive and consistently well written of the whole work, he describes the familiar signs by which the true Church can be identified—it is one, holy, universal, and apostolic. The explanation of each sign again bears within it an implicit reflection on the Calvinists' claims, and where need be, these claims are actually stated and countered.

Having described the nature of the Church, he now goes on, in the introduction to the second and longest part, to put forward the idea of the "rules of faith" that both govern the Church and distinguish it from a counterfeit society. The fundamental "rule" is God's Word, the Bible, the interpretation of which is the source of all contention, and which must necessarily be capable of explanation by the remaining "rules": tradition, authority, the teaching of the councils and of the Fathers, the primacy of the pope, and finally by miracles on the supernatural plane and by natural reason in the sphere of ordinary common sense. Together these eight factors provide infallible touchstones by which the true and the false can be told apart, "and if anyone wants to reduce all these rules to one, he could say that the sole rule by which we can truly believe is the Word of God preached by the Church of God."[12]

The whole of this central part is an impressive attempt to summarize the diverse aspects of the Church in a logically coherent, descriptive form. The author has really achieved here what he set himself to do: to make all the lines converge on one focal point. Each one of the forty articles, disposed in eight chapters, of which Chapter 1 on the Bible and Chapter 6 on the pope are the longest and the most significant, serves its precise function in building up a cumulative picture of the nature of the Church. This description is particularly striking in the light of the Second Vatican Council wherein old principles have found restatement in connection with the new decrees. Where the First Vatican Council was particularly impressed by his exposition of the role of the pope whose infallibility he quite simply assumed, we are perhaps less struck by the soundness of his doctrine, which is after all to be taken for granted in a Doctor of the Church, even when young; but what does appeal to us is his capacity for summarizing and stating doctrine simply and clearly. This is particularly true of his definitions of the role of councils (Chapter 4) and his exposition of the nature, function, and use of the Scriptures (Chapter 1). Even though some of his comments on vernacular translation of the Bible and the use of common tongues in the liturgy would raise a few official eyebrows today, this need not deter us from enjoying the amusing and competent way he states his case.[13]

The material in each chapter is again arranged in such a way as to refute the claims of the ministers step by step. It is noticeable, by the way, that Francis de Sales always attributes what he calls "violation of rules" directly to the leaders, never to the flock, because it was precisely his aim to drive a wedge between the leaders and the misled. It was an inconspicuous but most effective way of getting his opponents on his side, without their being properly aware of what was happening.

The third and last part, containing only two chapters of thirteen articles in all, remains a fragment, with the last few articles briefly worked out in what is little more than note form. As the ministers have left the union of the Church and violated all her rules, they are in no position to have clear views about the way her rules work out in practice, for an eye dissociated from the head cannot see the light, neither can the head see without eyes. This brings him to the discussion of some of the most vexed problems at issue: the sacraments, especially the Eucharist, confession, and marriage; the invocation of saints, the use of ritual, justification by faith or works, indulgences, the doctrine of merit, and finally, purgatory. All that he actually wrote of this was a preliminary discussion on the form of the sacraments and ten short articles on purgatory. In this preface he explains once more that he will continue to use the technique that has been his throughout: he will avail himself of the same source of proof as his adversaries; he will demonstrate from the Scripture itself the truth of every claim, more especially these very controversial ones, which were supposed to be so remote from the Bible. "I propose to limit myself as follows," he said. "The ministers will not fight except with the Scriptures—I agree; they only want to use those parts of the Scriptures which they can accept—I will conform to their wishes."[14] No single article of this work is without Scriptural references, each duly noted in the margin of the manuscript. Next in importance as a source are the Church Fathers, also admitted by the reformers, and then Luther, Calvin, and De Bèze themselves.[15]

Francis de Sales, it is said, broke off his work here because there was no longer any compelling need for it. After a year and a half, and now that he had the support of other missionaries, the conversion of the Chablais was beginning to be an accomplished fact. Even so, one cannot help feeling that the subject matter of this third part would have given less scope for the process of careful ordering and sifting of ideas and material provided in the first two sections. The topics now to be treated were also far more familiar and in a sense more straightforward than the ideas concerning the true nature of the Church that he had put at the basis of his *Meditations*. These points were the stock-in-trade of polemical interchange all over Europe; the last part would have been, in fact, hardly a meditation, but something more like plain controversy. One can then, perhaps, say that another reason why the work now lapsed was that the actual meditation, and what could best be worked out as a written treatise had come to a natural end. From this time onward, the spoken word, the sermon, attended now by those for whom it was meant, could take over.

The originality of the *Meditations* lies largely in their approach and structure, it has been said. It is hardly possible to prove this kind of statement without detailed comparisons, but perhaps a cursory one will serve to some extent. Francis de Sales repeatedly named Robert Bellarmine's *Controversies* as his chief source, a book written especially for missionaries who were in heretical lands without a library; but it is interesting that Francis did not take over his ordering of the material. Bellarmine's treatise is arranged in three volumes; the first begins with the Bible and tradition and goes on to Christ as the head of the Church with the pope as His representative ruling over the Church Militant, which is then described in its practice and in its constitution. The Church Suffering and Triumphant, purgatory and heaven, form a transition to the discussion of the sacraments in the second volume and to the problem of grace and justification in the third. This is what might be called the classical and traditional statement of the Catholic position. Francis de Sales' master, Antonio Possevino, in his *Bibliotheca Selecta* (1593), provides a long summary of Bellarmine in order to encourage the missionary to use and copy his method of approaching heretics.[16] He himself merely summarizes the doctrines or "atheisms," as he calls them, of the chief heresiarchs, without any attempt, in a work of quite different scope, to provide systematic refutation on a larger scale. It would be hard, therefore, to find an approach similar to that of Francis de Sales in his own time; and though not unsimilar in spirit, the very much more profound and formal treatise of Bossuet on the *Variations of Protestantism* is very different in content.

If the comparison is not too farfetched, one might point to the similarity of approach of a number of modern works, especially among those inspired by the climate of ideas surrounding the Second Vatican Council. Allowing for all differences of form and method, and for the fact that the modern author has of course had to take into account the history of the past three centuries and the most recent theologians of other Christian denominations, the general attitude of some modern meditations on *The Idea of the Church*[17] is more similar to that of Francis de Sales than his own book was to contemporary controversy. Bishop Butler discusses (in this order) the idea of the Church as a visible society, the witness to it of tradition, history, the councils, the Fathers (especially to Francis' own two favorites, Cyprian and Augustine), and of eschatological expectation. One would not expect stern strictures in this ecumenical age, but the modern equivalent of a patronizing and bland assumption of superiority is as completely absent from this work as polemical abuse was from that of Francis de Sales. In both works a level tone, as of one scholar and gentleman in conversation with another, is maintained throughout. For a Counter-Reformation missionary this was a remarkable, indeed an untimely, achievement. The subject matter of controversy, one may say, has not changed. Theologians are still trained along roughly similar lines, and yet one could hardly have chosen at random, say, an English theological work of the nineteenth century for comparison with Francis de Sales. One finds closer analogies to his approach in the mid-twentieth century, the ecumenical age.

Having examined the subject matter of the *Meditations* in outline, and more especially the systematic ordering of its content, we can approach its form. How did Francis de Sales write at this early stage of his career? How did he achieve his effects? And what was his own attitude to writing and to language as a means of expression and persuasion?

Before St. Francis de Sales was declared a Doctor of the Church, a number of petitions were sent in to the Holy See; among them was one from the Bollandists, whose apostolate is exclusively one of scholarship and writing. Together with other points they stressed Francis' extraordinary capacity to express himself on dogmatic, ascetic, and moral matters in such a way "as to be understood by the unlearned and not be despised by the learned." This they consider harder, in its way, than writing great works of theology, and something only achieved by the best and ablest writers.[18] In their own terms, and in the concepts of their time, his adversaries, too, paid homage to the saint's powers of expression. The local news sheet in the Chablais, *Le Bon Patriote*, which grossly abused Francis' fellow missionaries, confined itself to warning people from going anywhere near this dangerous man, the Provost de Sales who was an adept in all the arts of black magic and who could sway his hearers by the power of his "langue enchanteresse."[19] This may, perhaps, apply to his written word as well as to his persuasive speech.

Reading through this long and somewhat uneven work today, where the texture of the prose is so often broken up by Scriptural references and other quotations, it is not always easy to recapture the magic. There are arid tracts, but as one reads on, one finds there are also many rewarding surprises; certainly anyone who only knows this saint's writing from the *Introduction*, and the general reader is almost certainly in this category, will find it hard to believe that the *Meditations* were written by the same person no more than about a dozen years earlier. Where the one, on the surface at any rate, is all gentleness, flowered imagery, and long smooth periods, the other is full of energy, unadorned statement, and the cut and thrust of spare, logically determined sentences. The author's background of rhetorical training, which taught him to look on language as the art of persuasively communicating intellectual subject matter and of marshalling abstract ideas in order, is evident in every page of the *Meditations*. So is his more narrow legal training, which had provided him with the logical equipment to defend his case against an opponent.

But though evident on closer examination, these qualities are rarely obtrusive, for the whole art of a good rhetorician consisted in hiding the bony structure of his technique beneath an excellent style. Francis was able to meet the opponents, humanists for the most part, whose learning was almost an ingredient of their heresy, on their own ground and to fight with their weapons. One of the chief claims of the reformers was, after all, that they wrote so as to be understood by the people, whereas the Catholics, it was said, were content to argue among one another in scholastic Latin. The scholastic framework of Francis de Sales' theological thinking is, of course, present in the *Meditations*, but there again it is carefully camouflaged, for it was anathema to the Calvinists whom he was trying to win over. Syllogistic formulation has been almost completely avoided; it remains only in the rhetorical device of making the argument proceed by a series of questions. They are not, however, true rhetorical questions, implying the answer "No, of course not," or no answer at all, but simply a more vivid form of statement:

How did the Jews ever become God's people? By circumcision, a visible sign; and the rest of us? By Baptism, a visible sign . . . Who persecuted the synagogue? Egyptians, Babylonians, Philistines, all visible people. And the Church? Pagans, Turks, Moors, Saracens, heretics, all of them visible. Good God, and here we are, still asking: is the Church visible? But what is the Church? An assembly of men made of flesh and blood. And are we, then, to go on saying that the Church is just a spirit or a ghostly entity which looks as though it's visible but is only an illusion?[20]

Only the last of these questions, the climax of the argument, is truly rhetorical.

Francis de Sales does not overwork this device, or any of the techniques connected specifically with the spoken word, e.g., repetition, amplification, contrast, direct exhortation; he writes with a view to setting out his ideas plainly and in good order, preserving what he calls the "naifveté" and "suavité" of true meaning in an atmosphere of frankness and common sense, writing "à la bonne foy et franchement."[21] Straightforward exposition carries the main burden of the work:

God made our natural reason; and hates nothing that He has made, and as He has marked our understanding with His own light, we must not imagine that the supernatural light He gives to believers can be hostile and contrary to natural light; both come of the same Father, one naturally, the other in a more excellent and higher way; they should therefore stay together like two loving sisters. Whether in nature or above nature, reason always remains reasonable and truth true; thus it is the same eye that can see only two paces ahead in the gloom of a very dark night, that can also see the circle of a wide horizon by the lovely light of the noonday sun; the light is different, not the eye. And in the same way, truth is certainly always the same, whether in nature or above nature, but the light by which our intellect sees it varies; faith shows us what is above nature, intellect what is in nature, but truth is never contrary to itself.[22]

Francis de Sales could also write in a more conversational tone when his primary aim was not exposition, but the creation of an atmosphere, sometimes one of irony:

> And as to this habit of singing the psalms regardless of place and occupation, who can fail to see that this is holding religion in contempt? Isn't it an offense of the divine Majesty to use the exquisite words of the psalms without proper reverence and attention? And to say prayers as though one were simply chatting is surely a mockery of the one addressed. When, in Geneva or elsewhere, one sees a shop-boy playing about while he is singing these psalms, and breaking off the thread of a very beautiful prayer to say "What can I do for you, Sir?," isn't it clear that he is just using a means as an end and singing these divine songs quite simply to amuse himself, and this in spite of the fact that he believes them to be the work of the Holy Spirit? What an odd thing to hear the cook singing David's penitential psalms shouting at every verse for the bacon, the capon, the partridge. "The Psalmist's voice," says Des Montaignes (Book 1, ch. 56), "is too divine just to exercise the lungs and please the ear."[23]

The point here at issue was the popular use of Marot's very indifferent rhymed version of the psalms, this "rimaillerie," as Francis calls it. The thought leads him to one of his frequent epigrammatical formulations with a coined ironical word: "O you who pride yourselves on being able to sing and chant these "Marotted" French psalms, surely it would be better to be silent in Latin than to blaspheme in French."[24] Like Montaigne, whom he quotes repeatedly in these chapters, especially the essay entitled *Des Prières*, he disapproved strongly of what he called the "profanation" of the Scriptures and the liturgy when translated into the very changing and varied regional vernacular of even one single country. When it came to a Basque or Breton version of the New Testament, who was to be the judge of its accuracy, he asks with Montaigne.[25]

Often, he summarizes an argument with a telling picture or an anecdote: "That excellent theologian Robert Bellarmine heard from a very reliable source the story of a woman in England who listened to a minister reading our Chapter 25 of Ecclesiasticus (although they only consider it an ancient book and not canonical). And because there is talk in it of the wickedness of women, she got up and said: 'And that's supposed to be the Word of God? The devil's I should say.'"[26] Or in a more serious context he clinches an argument by calling up a picture of the way of life of missionaries, witnessing to the usefulness of religious orders and of the three vows:

> Who can ever blot out the glory of the many religious of every kind of order and of so many secular priests who freely left their own country or rather, their own world, and exposed themselves to wind and tide so as to reach the people of the New World and lead them to the true faith and bring them the light of the Gospel? And without any equipment except their lively trust in God's Providence, with nothing to look forward to except hard work, poverty and martyrdom, with no aim except to honour God and save souls, went straight off to make their home among cannibals, Canary Islanders, Negroes, Brazilians, Malayans, Japanese, and other foreign peoples; and there they lived as prisoners, living in exile from their own country in this world so that these poor people might not be banished from paradise in the next . . . dying as slaves to give those countries Christian liberty.[27]

The articles vary in the way they are constructed; some are carefully written and corrected, with many detailed stylistic improvements, one word being substituted for another to improve the rhythm,[28] the second version usually being firmer, more terse, and even elegant. It is this precision and firmness that make the style of the *Meditations* seem so much more modern than that of the *Introduction*, and more truly a forerunner of the far more neatly pruned and regular style of the French Academy, even pointing forward to Pascal.

The articles are of fairly uniform length, rarely more than about a thousand words, and are constructed according to a certain pattern which is, however, sufficiently varied not to become too noticeable. The opening paragraph consists either of an expository statement, like the one about natural reason quoted above, which may refer to the argument in the preceding article; or else the new subject matter is introduced by an illustrating quotation from the Bible, one of the Fathers, a council, if possible seeking a concrete image before the reader. This is developed by a point taken from the works of perhaps Calvin, Luther, or De Bèze; the matter is then argued in a series of questions and answers, which is often an imaginary dialogue of great vividness. There follows a brief exhortation, which merges into a summarizing final statement leading on to the next proposition in a further article. The general pattern can perhaps best be illustrated by an account of an actual article from the important central part of the work: *That we need some other rule besides the Word of God.*[29]

When Absalom wanted to revolt against his father he sat by the wayside and called out to passers-by that he was setting himself up as a just judge against the king. Many Absaloms line the roads of Germany and France. There is, for instance, Théodore de Bèze who argues in his book on the marks of the true Catholic Church (1592) that the interpretation of Scripture can only come out of the Scriptures themselves. We say "Amen" to this, but what about differing interpretations? Who is to judge between us? Now we come to question and answer:

> This is the big point, Christians, and now let us have a good look at the spirit of division that exists between us. Your people tell you to go back to the Scriptures; we are there before you ever came to be, and what we believe, we find there, plain and clear. But (you will say), it must be properly understood, each passage rightly related to every other and then to the Creed; that's what we have been trying to do for more than fifteen hundred years. You are all wrong about it, says Luther. Who told you? Scripture. What part of the Scriptures? Why, this part, and that, duly collated and

fitted to the Creed. On the contrary, I reply. It is you, Luther, who are wrong; the Scriptures tell me so in the following passage, carefully collated with this other part, and both taken in conjunction with the articles of faith. I don't question that we have to give credence to the Holy Writ; who doesn't know that it is in the highest degree credible? What is worrying me is how I am to understand the Scriptures, what conclusions and consequences are to be drawn from it; for these are varied, innumerable, and often contradictory on one and the same point; everyone then takes sides, some for, some against, and who will then show me the truth in all this fruitless argument? Who will show me Scripture in its true, native colors? For the colorful sheen on the neck of this dove looks different as often as those who are looking at it change their position and the place where they are standing. The Scriptures are a most holy and infallible touchstone, and whatever proposition stands this test I accept as faithful and sound.

There follows the exhortation:

Ah, anyone who says that our Lord has embarked us in His Church at the mercy of the wind and waves without giving us a skilled pilot who really knows the art of navigation and can read charts and use the compass, is in effect saying that God wants to destroy us. Even if He had given us the most excellent compass and the most accurate chart in the world, what use would they be unless there were someone who knew the infallibly right way to guide the ship? What's the use of a very good tiller if there is no captain to turn the helm according to the chart? But if everybody is allowed to turn it as he sees fit, who can fail to see that we are lost? It's not the Scriptures which need a rule and elucidation from outside, as De Bèze thinks we believe; no, it is rather our commentaries, conclusions, understandings, interpretations, conjectures, additions, and other such brain-children of man which need a ruling, for our minds cannot keep still and are always busy with new inventions. And certainly we want no judge to decide between us and God as De Bèze seems to infer in his *Letter;* we want a judge between a man like Calvin, De Bèze, Luther and, on the other hand, one like Eckius, Fisher and More; our concern is not whether God understands the Scriptures better than we do but whether Calvin understands them better than St. Augustine or St. Cyprian.[30]

After a quotation from St. Hilary and a further one from Luther he sums up the whole article in a final paragraph bringing an analogy from the function of the judge in civil law: although he works by means of the law, he stands outside it and above it when he applies its ruling: "If everybody is authorized to expound the meaning of the Holy Writ, difficulties become interminable, and if he who has authority to put forward an explanation can be in error, then we've got to begin all over again all the time. So there must be some infallible authority whose proposals we are bound to accept: God's Word cannot err, neither can he who proposes it, and settled in this way, everything will be perfectly safe and certain."[31] This ending then forms the bridge to the next very brief article, which suggests that the Church is meant to be, and is in fact, an infallible "rule" or guide. As in the scholastic framework, each article therefore is a link in a carefully welded logical chain, yet the transitions are so easy and the mechanism so well concealed beneath the easy sequence of lucid, almost conversational sentences, that the tautness of the argument to which one is all along being submitted comes as something of a surprise at the end. And the secret? ". . . estre bien espris de la doctrine qu'on enseigne et de ce qu'on persuade. Le souverain artifice c'est de n'avoir point d'artifice."[32]

Artifice is used here, not in the sense of "art" but of "artificial contrivance," and the *Meditations* certainly show Francis de Sales' art in the true sense of the term. The style of this early work has been characterized in general terms but never discussed in any detail.[33]

Some further features are perhaps here worth stressing. There are, it is true, very few images in the *Meditations* in comparison with the later works. Yet even the few passages quoted show that metaphorical parallels come to Francis de Sales perfectly naturally even at this state. They are not so much a deliberate technique of style, as in the *Introduction*, but a spontaneous instrument of thought, the swift illumination of an equivalence. The shimmering, shifting colors of the rock-dove's plumage are for him a real and meaningful equivalent of deceptive appearances which vary with the eye of the beholder, of God's Word which may sound different in every ear. The two metaphors which follow, that of the touchstone and of the ship without a pilot, though less personal than that of the dove, run through the whole work, appearing from time to time in an unforced way. To these might be added a third one, closely connected with the touchstone image: it is that of the false coiners who have debased the gold with alloy. The touchstone, which now that this object is no longer in common use, is a dead metaphor, was a vivid and valid comparison then. The variety of coins circulating in a much conquered territory like the Chablais gave every scope for forgers. The touchstone, a smooth, fine-grained piece of black jasper or dark quartz, against which suspected gold was rubbed and the resulting streak of color scrutinized, was in the pocket of every merchant who needed to tell true coins from false.[34] The "gentlemen of Thonon" were mostly merchants, and a buried treasure of moldy old coins hidden in a ruined house, abandoned after the devastating passage of armies, was not unfamiliar.

> But what happens when I have the following proposition in my hands: Our Lord's natural body is really, substantially, and actually present in the Blessed Sacrament of the altar. I test it by application, touching it at every point and angle against the expressed and most pure Word of God and the Apostles' Symbol of faith; there is no place where I don't rub it a hundred times, if you like, and the more I look at it, the more clearly I recognize it to be made of the finest gold and the purest metal. You say that you have done the same and find base metal in it. What

do you expect me to do? . . . who is to put us out of doubt? It's no good saying—the touchstone.

Oh well, you may answer, we haven't created a new church, we have just rubbed up and cleaned the old coins which had long lain hidden in ruined buildings and had got all dirty and black, disfigured with grime and mildew. But please don't go on saying that you own the metal and the stamping mold; the faith and the sacraments are surely necessary both one and the other. So you are false coiners unless you can show the power by which you claim to stamp such images on the king's coins. But let us go on: have you really purified this Church? Have you cleaned this coinage? Then show us what it looked like and the characters imprinted on it when it fell and was buried in the earth and began to gather mold. It fell, you say, in the time of St. Gregory or soon after. Say what you like, but at that time it had the character of miracles. Where is that now? If you cannot show us, and in detail, the inscription and image of the kind on your coins (and we can show it to you on ours)—then ours will pass as genuine and true in weight whereas yours, as alloyed and clipped, will be sent back to the melting pot.[35]

And again, on the edge of the wide expanse of Lac Léman where sudden and deadly storms were a familiar feature of their experience, the thought of an unpiloted ship at the mercy of the wind needed no great elaboration. Like the idea of being swindled, it struck home at once.

Everyone wants to embark in the ship of the Holy Spirit, but there is only one ship, and only this one ship will reach port, the rest are hurrying on to founder at the end. Ah, how great the danger if you make a mistake. Ah, how dangerous to be mistaken! All the captains speak with equal boasting and assurance, for they all say they are master navigators and this misleads most people.[36] And so you sail on, no needle, compass or rudder, across the ocean of human opinions, and all you can look forward to is an unhappy shipwreck. I implore you, now, while this day lasts, while God gives you the chance, cast yourselves into the saving bark of real repentance, commit yourselves to the happy ship which is bound full sail to the harbor of glory.[37]

The images were not new, but their atmosphere was "altogether Savoyard"; as Francis had promised, the language in which he spoke to people of the Chablais was their own, heard everyday in the streets of Thonon and in the marketplace. Francis advocates "un langage clair, naif, net";[38] his vocabulary, like the names which God gave to the apostles was "moelleux et massif"— full of marrow and strength; and with Montaigne he might have said: "un parler simple et naif, et tel sur le papier quà la bouche, un parler succulent et nerveux, court et serré . . . éloigné d'affectation, . . . Puisséje ne me servir que des mots qui servent aux halles à Paris."[39] Montaigne tells his readers that his is "un livre de bonne foy," and Francis de Sales says: "Prenez donques, Messieurs, en bonne part ce present que je vous fais,"[40] both from the beginning establishing a personal relationship with their readers, asking them to proceed "à la bonne foy et franchement."[41]

It is not intended to push this comparison too far; the two works in question are too completely different in kind and so were their authors. Yet it remains a striking fact that Montaigne is the only non-theological writer whom Francis quotes; he had read him, he used him as an authority in evidence on a matter concerning language, he would not have done this had he not found him both revealing and sympathetic as a writer. He was drawn to him not only as an artist, a fellow humanist, but as one sharing his deep psychological interest in man. There is no call to speak of influence, but one may stress a certain similarity of atmosphere, that of informality and directness. Both writers appeal, in their way, and with their different purpose, to the common sense and experience of their readers. It is possible, too, to show an actual verbal assimilation of Montaigne in the articles in which Francis cites him; he even owes to him (a point not noted) the famous shop-boy and the cook in the passages quoted above and by the saint's biographers in every passing mention of the *Controversies*.

At the time when Francis de Sales' writings were being scrutinized before the title of Doctor of the Church was conferred on him in 1877, the devil's advocate picked out as an objection his habit of quoting from Montaigne, "not only a profane (i.e. not theological) but also an irreligious and immoral writer."[42] The promoters countered this by pointing out that the Fathers also quoted freely from contemporary writers. They might further have said that the only essay Francis used for direct quotation was the most religious of them all, that called *Des Prières*, where Montaigne makes a moving submission to the Church in which, as he says, "I die and was born." Far from sharing the apprehension of the devil's advocate, we have every reason to be grateful to the chance which put Montaigne's essays into the hands of Francis de Sales and helped him to leaven the solid mass of doctrine that he had to put before the gentlemen of Thonon, making his "present" to them one of the first readable books on a sacred subject in the French language.

NOTES

1. See *Oeuvres*, 1:lxxxviii, cxiii.

2. *Lettre* 42 (Oeuvres, 11:108). The editors have translated this as: "Je roule en mon esprit des Méditations sur les mutations des H´rétiques de notre temps," seeming to make the work into a precursor of Bossuet's *Variations du Protestantisme* 16. A more recent edition of Francis de Sales' work retains both his own titles and has dropped the official but inaccurate one: S. François de Sales, *Mémorial sur l'Église,* Ire partie des *Méditations,* and *Mémorial sur les règles de la foi,* 2e et 3e parties des *Méditations,* edited by Louis-François Dechevis, 2 vols. (Namur, 1958 and 1960).

3. *Lettre* 544 (*Oeuvres*, 14:191), 17 August 1609.

4. The Montaigne scholar, Fortunat Strowski, *Saint François de Sales,* 2nd edition (Paris, 1928), 77.

5. Letter to his Metropolitan, Pierre de Villars, 15 February 1609, *Lettre* 514 (*Oeuvres*, 14:126).

6. See *Oeuvres*, 1:cxxix onwards. The amount of editorial work that was done on this text, and not always accounted for in the apparatus, can best be judged by a comparison of the Table of Contents of the Annecy edition of the text and that of the English translation of 1886. One of the most important chapters of the book (Part I, ch. 3, The Marks of the Church) was originally placed halfway through Part II, and some of the individual articles were variously disposed in relation to one another, and also divided up differently.

7. *Oeuvres*, 4:15-20.

8. *Oeuvres*, 1:413-19.

9. *Controverses*, Avant-Propos (*Oeuvres*, 1:13).

10. Ibid. (*Oeuvres*, 1:13).

11. Ibid. (*Oeuvres*, 1:15).

12. *Controverses* 2, Avant-Propos (*Oeuvres*, 1:147).

13. *Controverses*, 2:1:7-9 (*Oeuvres*, 1:179-187).

14. *Controverses*, 3, Avant-Propos (*Oeuvres*, 1:346).

15. For a list of his sources, Catholic and heretical, see the editor's preface to the *Controversies, Oeuvres* 1:cxxxvii-cxliii. The English reader will be interested to notice that Francis de Sales quotes several times from St. Edmund Campion's *Rationes decem redditae academicis Angliae* (Ingolstadt, 1584), Nicholas Sanders' *De visibili monarchia Ecclesiae* (Louvain, 1571), and Thomas Stapleton's *Promptuarium Catholicum super omnia Evangelia totius anni* (Louvain, 1591). He also mentions St. John Fisher.

16. Antonio Possevino, *Bibliotheca Selecta*, 459.

17. By B. C. Butler, now Bishop Butler, formerly Abbot of Downside (London, 1962).

18. Quoted by Dom Mackey in the preface to his translation of *The Catholic Controversy*, Library of St. Francis de Sales, Vol. 3 (London, 1886), viii.

19. Mackey, Preface (*Oeuvres*, 1:cxxvii).

20. *Controverses*, 1:2:1 (*Oeuvres*, 1:47).

21. *Controverses*, 2:6:2 (*Oeuvres*, 1:236).

22. *Controverses*, 2:8:1 (*Oeuvres*, 1:330-331).

23. *Controverses*, 2:1:9 (*Oeuvres*, 1:186).

24. *Controverses*, 2:1:5 (*Oeuvres*, 1:175).

25. *Controverses*, 2:1:7 (*Oeuvres*, 1:180).

26. *Controverses*, 2:1:8 (*Oeuvres*, 1:184).

27. *Controverses*, 1:3:11 (*Oeuvres*, 1:119).

28. *Controverses*, 2, Avant-Propos (*Oeuvres*, 1:142-43).

29. *Controverses*, 2:3:1 (*Oeuvres*, 1:202-209).

30. *Controverses*, 2:3:1 (*Oeuvres*, 1:205-207).

31. *Controverses*, 2:3:1 (*Oeuvres*, 1:208-209).

32. From the letter on preaching, addressed to Archbishop André Frémyot, brother of Madame de Chantal, 5 October 1604. *Lettre* 229 (*Oeuvres*, 12:321).

33. Mackey, Preface (*Oeuvres*, 1:cxxiv). "[I]es qualités de naturel, de beauté, de force et de persuasion . . . nulle part dans les oeuvres de notre Saint, on ne rencontre une telle énergie, une confiance aussi inébranlable . . ." "La langue est très pure, très française . . . Les *Controverses* prouvent l'universel triomphe du style régulier, élégant et périodique avant Balzac et l'académie française" (Strowski, 74). "Son style, tout simple, tout jaillissant, est l'expression même de sa pensée; il est du terroir, comme le vin des vignes chablaisiennes . . . Il passe en effet dans ces feuilles une intime allégresse qui vient à l'auteur du sentiment de sa force, de sa paix, de la valeur et de la transcendance de sa foi catholique" (Francis Trochu, S. *François de Sales*, 2 vols. [Paris, 1955] 1:345). "The style is spare, rapid and full of immediacy, of a secret energy consistently kept up from the first line to the last. The writing is close to the classical prose of the 17th century . . ." (Antonio Mor, *San Francesco di Sales, Scrittore* [Rome: Editrice Studium, 1960], 51). "Ce n'est que du solide journalisme religieux" (J. Calvet, *La littérature religieuse de saint François de Sales à Fénelon* [Paris, 1928], 25).

34. The figurative use of "touchstone," at any rate in England, goes back to 1533.

35. *Controverses*, 1:3:7 (*Oeuvres*, 1:107).

36. *Controverses*, 1:2:6 (*Oeuvres*, 1:74).

37. *Controverses*, 2:8:4 (*Oeuvres*, 1:342).

38. *Lettre* 229 (*Oeuvres*, 12:322).

39. Pléiade edition, 1:25.

40. *Controverses*, Avant-Propos (*Oeuvres*, 1:6).

41. *Controverses*, 2:6:2 (*Oeuvres*, 1:236).

42. Quoted by Dom Mackey in the preface to his translation, xxi.

III

The Art of the Writer

It is a commonplace in the history of spirituality to say that St. Francis de Sales was a pioneer in sounding the universal call to holiness and in bringing true devotion among the people. But this statement needs a little further investigation, for the strengthening of individual and personal piety was, after all, fundamental to the thought of the Counter Reformation in general. The movement of bringing committed prayerfulness out of the cloister into the world had been going on fairly intensively for most of the sixteenth century, in the later half of which Francis de Sales was born (21 August 1567). It was one of the answers to the Protestant charge in general, and to Luther's specific accusation that the split between the so-called life of perfection and that of the ordinary Christian was unwarranted; according to Luther, the idea of establishing orders for "religious" (the very word pointed to a misconception) rested on false assumptions.

The Catholic countermove to these in part quite justified charges left its mark on the spiritual literature of the later part of this century in countless primers, books of devotion and meditation, ways of perfection and spiritual emblem books which would never have achieved their great diffusion if they had been designed only for "religious." For concrete proof, if we want one from our own history of spirituality, we need only turn to a bibliography of English recusant literature which includes translations from all the great Spanish and French handbooks of the time. Indeed, the very fact that these works were written in what was still, after all, regarded as the vernacular at that time, is a clue to the true nature of the books and of the readers, that is to say, the lay people (apart, it is true, from cloistered nuns) whom they were designed to reach. As for France, a glance at Jean Dagens' interesting bibliography at once disproves the commonly held assumption that Francis de Sales' *Introduction to the Devout Life* had any primacy.[1]

But even though the *Introduction* was by no means first in the field, it is true that Francis himself takes care to define the audience he is seeking to address. He is not writing, he says, for the cloistered few in the first instance, but for "those who live in cities within their families and surrounded by household cares, for people at court or in the press of public affairs."[2] At the same time, he points out that "it is a mistake, indeed a heresy [surely a strong word in this context] to want to banish the devout life from among the soldier's battalions, the workman's shop, the courts of princes, the homes of married people."[3] And how did he define devotion? ". . . it is, in fact, love, though it has many aspects . . . it is a spiritual alertness and liveliness which makes us fall in promptly and wholeheartedly with the demands of charity . . . it is a more excellent charity, moving us to do as much good as we can, and to do it swiftly and willingly, going beyond commands to what is counseled or inspired."[4]

If, then, it was heretical not to do what Francis de Sales is generally thought to have initiated, the secret of his revolutionary influence on his time, and indeed on people all over the world for the past four hundred years, cannot lie in the mere scope and content, or the message, of his work. He himself gives us the answer: "I am incapable of saying anything in this introduction which has not already been said before; this is not my intention nor ought I to try. Here you have the same flowers as of old, my dear reader; but the posy will be new simply because I have arranged and presented it differently."[5]

It was not so much what he said that struck a new chord but the personal, intimate way in which he said it, taking the reader to his heart from the first, speaking to him as to a well-known friend and quite simply assuming that the love of God was the only thing that mattered. His characteristic gift lay in his method of ordering and presenting familiar material, bringing it home with unerring psychological insight and revealing his own personality—his warmth, sympathy, intelligence and humor—in his way of writing, in his style in the widest sense of that word. He takes a high place in the small group of saints and doctors of the Church—Jerome, Augustine, Thomas Aquinas, John of the Cross—who all in their different way are theologians, mystics, philosophers and teachers but at the same time artists in their own right, combining literary gifts with the capacity to express and teach something personal and therefore new about the relationship of the human person with God. The teaching was new precisely because it was an essentially personal synthesis. In the case of St. Francis de Sales this is not always sufficiently stressed, perhaps because the artist never intrudes himself and is there exclusively to aid the pastor and teacher.

This capacity to conceal his art, especially in his preaching, was noted by the most perceptive of his early biographers, his Cistercian friend, Dom Jean de Saint François, who says:

> He had a strong, calm and deliberate voice, his style was pleasing, his words well chosen, apt and simple, matching the quality of his thought which was clear, ordered and in no way confused or intricate. His concepts were lofty and divine but he expressed them so intelligibly and easily that everyone grasped his meaning, right down to the simplest listener who found it easy to remember the sermon because the method of preaching was so straightforward and the substance of it so perfectly arranged and disposed. A few ignorant people, not understanding how difficult it is to achieve this effect of simplicity, imagined they could have done as well as he did; but this is precisely the highest degree of excellence in a public speaker—making his audience think it is all quite easy.[6]

Although, then, the *Introduction* was by no means the first book of its kind, it was the first one, certainly in the emergent French language of the early seventeenth century, which was of high literary value. Sainte-Beuve called Francis de Sales the Montaigne of spiritual literature, and the comparison remains valid. He was the first to give the language of devotion all the charm of familiar colloquy without depriving it of dignity. Writing in the manner of the best secular authors of his time (he read Montaigne when a number of the Essays were first published in 1580), Francis expounded doctrine, analyzed the human passions and the whole range of psychological attitudes, influenced the will by a subtle, highly differentiated art of persuasion—and all this in the language of everyday life, in an idiom which fully expressed his own temperament as a humanist, an artist, a man of the world accomplished in "civilité."

From the various drafts and editions of the *Introduction* we can see what a scrupulously careful writer he was: there are over two thousand amendments between one edition and the next, and most revealing of all, the author made some changes in the order of the chapters within the three sections of the first edition and the subsequent arrangement in five sections as the work has come down to us. The right and wholly logical ordering of material, as a study of the comparative tables of the Annecy edition of the works shows, was a matter of vital concern to the author; in the end, the careful inner balance of the instruction is perfectly reflected in the harmony and symmetry of its outer form, a sequence of brief chapters grouped, as it seems, naturally and inevitably. In easy stages Philothea is shown how to make a beginning in the devout life which is first of all defined; then she is taught to pray and make the best use of the sacraments, practice the virtues proper to her state, and again, these are defined and described in action. Finally she is put on guard against temptations and shown how to renew her resolutions and newly won insights in a steady effort of annual review. The style is even, leisurely; important points are reinforced by parallels and images mostly drawn from nature, from family life, but also, with deliberate naivety, from the medieval world of bestiary and fable. Philothea learns by familiar terms of reference and in a pleasing way. The imagery that may prove a stumbling block now when the parallels are less familiar was an important spiritual aid to understanding in the world of the late Renaissance, making abstract concepts plain and memorable without diminishing them.

In Francis de Sales' next work, *Treatise on the Love of God* (1616), the same process of explanation and instruction is continued, but spiritual truth is analyzed at a deeper level. He is still writing for lay people, but for those who have been living in the spirit of the *Introduction*, and this includes more especially Madame de Chantal and the newly founded Order of the Visitation. Theotimus, the soul in love with God, has replaced Philothea; the theme is the development of the mystical life, the relationship of love between the human person and God unfolding, flowering and bearing fruit in the human soul. The work is far more complex and comprehensive in scope than the first, but in spite of the original and less familiar train of thought, it has the same firmness of logical structure to draw it together, the opening books showing the origins of the mystical life and the laws that govern it, the central section describing the state of union towards which this love tends, and in the end, as is reasonable while the soul is still "in via," going back to the beginning, to the simple practice of day by day virtues from which no mystical ecstasy can dispense the lover. The style to some extent reflects the greater complexity of the subject matter; the imagery is less exuberant and manifold, giving place, often, to parables of poetic beauty which express what lies beyond the conscious realm. For Francis de Sales, the human person's love of God is above all something in the will, far above feelings and sense concepts. But the *Treatise* clothes these concepts in concrete terms wherever possible, dealing with intangibles in a way that makes them readily understandable on both the logical and intuitive plane. "God had flooded the center of his soul, or its summit, to use his own expression, with such brilliant light that he saw the truths of the faith and their excellence with an unclouded vision," said Madame de Chantal in a letter of 1623 to Dom Jean de Saint François. "He used such precise and easily understood terms that he made people grasp very readily the most delicate and subtle truths of the spiritual life."[7]

In this fourth centenary year of St. Francis de Sales' birth I should also like to draw attention to an earlier and less well-known work which seems to me a good example of his powers to state old truths in a new and creative way: *Meditations on the Church*.[8] They were initially based on a series of talks planned for the Calvinists of the Chablais region on the southern banks of Lac Léman where he worked as a missionary from 1594 to 1598. The elders, or the "Gentlemen of Thonon," as he calls them throughout the work, had sworn on oath never to listen to him and had forbidden his sermons to their flock. Francis then wrote a weekly news sheet, eighty articles in all, none longer than two or, at the most, three sides, explaining the nature of the Church to the elders, all of whom were personally known to him, some from his childhood spent in the Chablais; they were men of great piety, well versed in the Scriptures without being erudite. He never talks down to them, never attacks them personally, addressing them as "separated brothers," an unheard of courtesy in that age of fierce polemics. He turned to them as to friends and pleaded for a hearing: "You will have read better and more complex things but please do stop to have a look at this: it is really Savoyard, and it is very salutary to come home for a breath of your own native air for a change," he says—an allusion to the fact that heresies were imported from abroad as far as Savoy was concerned, that is, from France and Germany. "Needle and thread are my own, and little more; all I have had to do is to unpick the garment and then sew it up again in my own way."[9] He can only teach what he himself has learnt, but he will try and put it in a "new way."

He starts with the concrete situation: who authorized your ministers? What is a church? What are the characteristics of a true church, what part do the Scriptures play in it, tradition, the councils, the Fathers, the pope, the witness of miracles and natural reason? Which are the true sacraments, what can we really believe about the afterlife and purgatory? This is as far as the news sheets go. The general plan of the work emerges as simple, clear, bold and wholly original when compared with other works of controversy at that time, for instance, that of Bellarmine which Francis de Sales consulted freely. Its originality, one might even say, its modernity, lies in its structure and its approach.

In the first part Francis shows what signs distinguish the true Church, in Part II (the longest) he describes the rules of faith by which the Church lives, in the last, unfinished part he proposed to demonstrate the working out of these rules in practice. The clarity of this scheme, designed by a mind of legal training, is in itself greatly satisfying, the more so as the plan nowhere obtrudes itself; it emerges naturally with the progress of ideas, conferring a sense of order and harmony which is the distinguishing mark of everything Francis de Sales wrote. At the same time it is the first attempt at an informal work of theology written in the French language, and had it been published when it was written, it would quite conceivably have had a liberating influence on theological writing comparable with that of Montaigne's work in the secular sphere. Francis writes with a view to setting out his ideas plainly and in good order, basing himself on the spoken word and preserving what he calls the "naifveté" and "suavité" of true meaning in an atmosphere of openness and common sense, writing "à la bonne foy et franchement." Straightforward exposition carries the main burden of the work:

> God made our natural reason; He hates nothing He has made, and as He has marked our understanding with His own light, we must not imagine that the supernatural light which faith gives us can be hostile and contrary to natural light. Both come from the same Father, one naturally, the other in a more excellent and higher way; they should therefore stay together like two loving sisters. Whether in nature or above nature, reason always remains reasonable, and truth true. Thus it is the same eye that can only see two paces ahead in the gloom of a very dark night and can yet descry the circle of a wide horizon by the lovely light of the noonday sun—the light is different, not the eye. And in the same way, truth is certainly always the same, whether in nature or above nature, but the light by which our intellect sees it may vary; faith shows us what is above nature, intelligence what is in nature, but truth is never contrary to itself.[10]

Then there is the more conversational tone when the primary aim is not exposition but the creation of an atmosphere, sometimes one of good-natured irony:

> And as to this habit of singing the psalms regardless of place and occupation, surely this amounts to holding religion in contempt? . . . When one sees shop-boys in Geneva and elsewhere fooling about while singing these psalms, and breaking off the thread of a very

beautiful prayer to call out: "What can I get for you, Sir?," isn't it clear that they are confusing means and ends and singing these divine songs quite simply for fun? How odd to hear the cook caroling David's penitential psalms and punctuating every verse with a call for the bacon, the partridge, the capon! . . . O you who pride yourselves on being able to sing these "Marotted" French psalms [Marot was the name of the very indifferent translator], surely it would be better to be silent in Latin than to blaspheme in French![11]

Francis de Sales' description of the nature of the Church in the forty articles which make up the central part of the *Meditations* is particularly striking if read at the present time when old principles have found restatement in connection with new decrees. Where the First Vatican Council was much impressed by the saint's exposition of the role of the pope—whose infallibility he quite simply assumed—we are perhaps no less struck by the soundness of his doctrine than by his capacity to summarize and state it in a way which does not seem to have dated. This is especially true of his definition of the role of councils (II, 4) and his exposition of the nature, function and use of the Scriptures (II, 1). Even though some of his comments on the use of the vernacular in the liturgy might raise a few official eyebrows today, this need not deter one from relishing the amusing and convincing way he states his case, especially when one considers the situation historically: there was as yet no true standard "vernacular." All in all, those who only know Francis de Sales by his later works will read the *Meditations* with astonishment. His manner of writing is bare and incisive, every word is weighed in the balance of logical aptness and economy. The logic is still there later on, in the *Introduction*, the *Treatise* and no less even in the letters, but it is more concealed within the firm articulation and structure which underlies the pleasing form.

Before St. Francis de Sales was declared a Doctor of the Church in 1877, the Bollandist Fathers, among many others, had sent their petition to the Holy See. As a particular point in the saint's favour they stressed his extraordinary capacity to express and expound dogmatic, ascetical and mystical matters in such a way "as to be understood by the unlearned and yet not be despised by the learned." This they considered harder in its way than writing works of profound theology, and they pointed to it as something only achieved by the ablest and most gifted writers. *Le Bon Patriote*, the news sheet of the Calvinists in the Chablais at the time of Francis' mission, put this in another way, more in harmony with the concepts of the age: they simply accused him of black magic and of having put a spell on his audience by the power of his "langue enchanteresse." His magic lay—to no small extent—in his art as a writer, and this is why, sanctity apart, he managed to influence minds and hearts so deeply, making true devotion acceptable to people in every walk of life.

NOTES

1. *Bibliographie chronologique de la littérature de spiritualité et de ses sources* (Paris, 1952). Between 1600 and 1608 alone, the year the *Introduction* was published, Dagens records some thirteen pages of titles.

2. *Introduction*, Preface.

3. *Introduction*, Part 1, ch. 3.

4. *Introduction*, Part 1, ch. 1.

5. *Introduction*, Preface.

6. *La vie du bien-heureux Messire François de Sales* (Paris, 1624), 150-51.

7. *St. Francis de Sales: A Testimony by St. Chantal*, newly edited in translation with an introduction by Elisabeth Stopp (London/Hyattsville, 1967), 166, 171.

8. This unfinished work was not published in Francis' lifetime. I have used the title by which he himself in his letters referred to what later became known as *Les Controverses*. It was used as evidence in the second canonization process and for this purpose was given a title which the author never used or intended. It has been republished in modern French as *Mémorial sur l'Église*, 1ʳᵉ partie des *Méditations*, and *Mémorial sur les règles de la foi*, 2ᵉ et 3ᵉ parties des *Méditations*, edited by Louis-François Dechevis, 2 vols. (Namur, 1958 and 1960).

9. *Controverses*, Avant-Propos (*Oeuvres*, 1:15, 13).

10. *Controverses*, 2:8:1 (*Oeuvres*, 1:330-31).

11. *Controverses*, 2:1:9, 2:1:5 (*Oeuvres*, 1:186, 175).

IV

HEALING DIFFERENCES:
ST. FRANCIS DE SALES IN SEVENTEENTH-CENTURY ENGLAND

"To read of St. Ignatius of Loyola or of St. Philip Neri or of St. Francis de Sales," wrote a perceptive yet kindly critic of the Church, "is to be aware that the Roman Church was possessed by a zeal for spiritual and moral reform as great as that of the Protestants of Northern Europe, and by a vocation to prayer and holiness which the Protestants barely understood. Yet some of the uncatholic tendencies of the Middle Ages were continued and even deepened in the revival that was led and organized by the Council of Trent."[1]

When the present essay was being written, a large picture-poster of the man who made this comment adorned many of the notice boards in St. Francis de Sales' mountain diocese, at Annecy, in Geneva itself, and especially in the Chablais region where the saint's presence is still so very much alive. Our critic was seen in conversation with Pope Paul VI in Rome in 1966. He was Dr. Ramsey, then Primate of the Anglican Communion. In the book in question he develops the idea that the Counter Reformation, in spite of its heroic achievement in "witnessing anew to the supernatural" yet failed, as a whole, to comprehend the true meaning of Luther's challenge and thus never quite recovered its catholicity. Yet from this stricture he excepts three of the greatest saints who put the principles of Trent into practice, stressing their zeal for reform and their call to prayer and holiness, which were, after all, truly "catholic," and in their time pointed forward to results now hoped for from the Second Vatican Council.

Dr. Ramsey's attitude toward St. Francis de Sales may be taken as representative of the Anglican viewpoint on him through the century we are considering. Of all the Counter-Reformation saints he was singled out in England as the guide *par excellence* to the devout life, the common ground of all Christians. Where much served to divide, he united. And this is still his meaning for us. As for English Catholics, they have felt deeply at home with him from the beginning, and his influence, spiritual and devotional rather than theological, and therefore in this sense perhaps rather restricted, has always been important, though in an unspectacular way: he simply forms part of our spiritual landscape. In his study of English Catholicism Bishop David Mathew concludes by saying that what we need most to illumine and revitalize our standards as Christians in a pagan world is, quite simply, "a new . . . St. Francis de Sales."[2]   There is no further explanation; it is taken for granted that the reader knows just what St. Francis stands for.

It is the task of this essay to try to describe how he has come to mean to us what he does in fact mean, and what part he has played in English devotional life, Catholic and Anglican. This investigation will center on the seventeenth century, which is the most interesting as well as the least explored. It was then that the foundations of St. Francis de Sales' reputation in England were laid among Catholics and Protestants alike while the later centuries saw a fuller development but hardly a change.

England meant only one thing to St. Francis de Sales: it was the land for which Catholic martyrs were shedding their blood so that it might return to the true faith. The years of his early manhood coincided with the peak point of the Elizabethan persecutions, and while he was studying in Paris he came into contact with English and Scottish Jesuits who were teaching at Clermont. They played an important part in the life of the college: it was a Scot, James Tyrie (1543-1597), a professor from Clermont, who was elected to represent the French Jesuit province at Rome on the committee of six who worked out the first printed version of the *Ratio Studiorum* published in 1586.[3] In 1587, the year before Francis left Paris, Mary Queen of Scots was executed at Fotheringay, an event which caused the greatest consternation in French court circles, where she was considered a daughter of France. All the Lorraines went into official mourning, in which Francis would have shared closely, as his father had attached him to the household of the duke of Mercoeur who was Philip Emmanuel of Lorraine. Mary Stuart was looked upon as a martyr to her faith, and the plight of her co-religionists was publicized that same year in a gruesome fashion in the Quartier Latin with an exhibition of their varied forms of torture and death. These pictures were displayed in the cemetery cloisters of the church of Saint Sévérin, a little way down the rue Saint Jacques from Clermont College.[4] None of the broadsheets and colored prints of this show seem to have been preserved, but judging by some of their counterparts still extant from German Reformation polemics, the exhibition certainly did not lack realism of a kind to affect even the most hardened, let alone the vulnerable, as the nineteen-year-old student, Francis de Sales, was at this time. At Padua too, at the college where his director, Antonio Possevino, taught, there were English Jesuits, and here Francis and his brother Gallois, who was at school there, would have met English university students, particularly medicals, of whom there were quite a large number at this time. Francis himself attended medical lectures.

It can be said, then, that England was a reality for Francis from his school days and that her people were always included in his prayer. "I declare it to be common knowledge," said St. Chantal in her canonization testimony in 1628, "that our Blessed Father had a great longing to go to England and convert this country. The English were close to his heart, and he wrote somewhere that he prayed for them most lovingly every day, asking God to gather them together again into the one true fold."[5]

Some years after the publication of the *Introduction* (1609), Marie de Médicis, the widow of Henry IV and at that time the regent of France, who had been greatly impressed by Francis' preaching at court in 1602, sent a richly bound and jeweled copy of the book to King James I of England. The King had a strong and well informed interest in theology; having read the book, he at once realized its quality and is said to have carried it about his person for several weeks, at the same time expressing his desire to meet the author. When St. Francis was told of this, he replied: "I would give my life a thousand times over to bring England back to the fold, but of course our Holy Father, the pope, would have to be pleased to send me on this mission."[6]

In the last two years of his life, a further, and this time a personal and unhappy link was formed with England. In 1620 Denis de Granier, a member of his own cathedral chapter of Geneva, who was furthermore a nephew of his former bishop, fled to the court of James I and formally apostatized in England. "There he is," wrote Francis in a letter expressing his strong personal grief, "cut off from the rest of the world by the sea, and from the Church by schism and error. Tell him," he goes on, showing that geographically speaking, England was a very remote, sea-girt land to him, "that all the waters of the English seas will never put out the fire of my love for him . . . I have a specially strong love for this great island and its king, and I never cease praying His Divine Majesty for its conversion, and with every confidence that my prayers will be answered as there are so many souls praying with me for this same end."[7] It is known that the saint did severe penance for his friend and that soon after Francis' death Denis de Granier did in fact leave England and return to the Church, wayward in his character ever after, but faithful at least to his religion.

Although this cannot, of course, be proved, it may well have been a useful recommendation for Denis de Granier arriving in England in 1620 that he was a former canon of the chapter of Francis de Sales, Bishop of Geneva. For by that time the name of the author of the *Introduction to the Devout Life* was already quite well known in this country, and not only among Catholics. Writing in August of that same year to the Jesuit Antoniotti, of Turin, who had sent for the saint's approval his translation into Italian of the *Introduction*, Francis said: "As to the *Introduction*, it is a fact that it has proved very useful (*utilissima*) in France, in Flanders, in England, and has had more than forty new impressions in French in various places; it has helped, too, to convert heretics."[8] "Even Huguenots," said St. Chantal in her testimony, "have a very high regard for those parts of the book which concern morals and the good life."[9]

The first recusant translation of the book appeared in 1613; a Protestant adaptation of the same work followed three years later, by which time the Catholic one had already reached its third edition. There had also been two Latin translations, at least one of which is known to have been read by Anglicans, who were also, for the most part, especially the ladies in court circles, capable of reading French devotional works and novels at that time.[10] Judging by what is known of James I, he was unlikely to have carried a book in his pocket without submitting it to detailed theological analysis and discussion with his courtiers, a captive audience. His own knowledge of French was excellent; as James VI of Scotland and the son of Mary Queen of Scots, he had been brought up in Edinburgh where French influence was strong. It is true that his education had been strictly Protestant, but his interest in religion was so great that he avidly read and appraised whatever came his way and whatever its slant. He was, moreover, a far more tolerant and humane person than either of his predecessors, Mary Tudor and Elizabeth, on the English throne. What was the religious atmosphere in England like when he and when his son, Charles I, succeeded to the throne, and who were the people, Catholic and Anglican, who were likely to have read St. Francis de Sales in Stuart times?

The last decade of Queen Elizabeth's reign had seen a slight improvement in the situation of Catholics in that the persecutions were less intensive, but two years after the accession of James I the Gunpowder Plot of 1605 again roused public hatred and exacerbated the penal laws against papists: their complete exclusion from all useful employment in civic life; the crippling fines for non-attendance at Protestant services, which could only be paid by the wealthiest; the atmosphere of danger and concealment in which they had to perform their religious duties; the imprisonment, torture, and execution of recognized priests and those who harbored them. The conditions of their life forced Catholics in upon themselves and made the deepening of the inward and spiritual life of each individual the first concern of their pastors. This in turn led to a relatively high number of vocations to the religious and priestly life; priests were trained at the English seminary at Douay, and in the Benedictine, Jesuit, and Franciscan houses in the Low Countries and in France, while an increasing number of girls went to join English communities overseas, devoted to teaching, or, more generally, to the contemplative life. There were Carmelites, Benedictines, Franciscans,

Dominicans. As the agitation after the plot died down and there was a slight relief of pressure, the Catholics in England embarked on what was probably their most peaceful era since the beginning of the Reformation. It lasted until the outbreak of the Civil War in 1842 which nevertheless gave them the semblance of a new corporate life; they were able to join in with the Anglicans against the Puritans and rally more openly around Charles I and his Catholic queen who were being persecuted in the name of religion.

It was among the exiled communities that Francis de Sales first became known to English men and women, and it was they who first translated his works for the benefit of their relatives at home and also to use within their own communities. The first English translation of the *Introduction* appeared at Douay in 1613 with the imprimatur of Dom Leander a San Martino, the president of the English Benedictines.[11] It was the work of "I.Y.," who has been identified by Dom Mackey as John Yaworth, O.S.B., by others, on insufficient evidence, as John Yakesley or John Yates. His translation, on the whole faithful and readable, rapidly went through a number of reprints (1614, 1615, 1617, 1622) and three, possibly four editions, the "last edition," as it was inscribed, being dated Paris, 1637. The translation was based on Francis' 1610 text and not on the "édition princeps" of 1608-09.

Within three years of its appearance, Yaworth's translation was pirated in an anonymous Protestant adaptation[12] that was printed by Nicholas Okes of St. Paul's Churchyard, one of the main publishing centers in London. Religious publishing enjoyed a great vogue in Stuart England. Of the 130 books, for instance, entered at the Stationers' Hall in the year of Denis de Granier's apostasy (1620), over half were religious in subject matter, and most of these devotional. But the other, unofficial editions of the *Introduction* were printed either at Rouen, Douay, or else, as this was frequently a cover-up imprint, at secret presses in England where men risked their lives, or at least their liberty, to provide Catholics with new spiritual reading matter. The first translation into any foreign language of the *Treatise on the Love of God* was made by Miles Car and published at Douay in 1630;[13] an English Benedictine nun of Cambrai, identified by some as Dame Agnes More, was responsible for the translation of the *Entretiens*, the

Delicious Entertainments of the Soule which came from Douay in 1632, that is, within three years of its appearance in France. Like that of the *Treatise*, this was the first translation into any foreign language.[14]

No other works of St. Francis de Sales appeared in translation until the second half of the nineteenth century; nor was there any printed account of his life until the English priests of Tournai College in Paris produced a revised translation of the *Introduction* in 1648, which was prefaced by a brief outline of his life.[15] There do not seem to have been any repercussions in England of St. Francis' canonization in 1665, but ten years later the Tournai translation was reprinted in Paris, then in London in 1688 by order of the Catholic King James II for the private use of his household.[16] Neither the *Treatise* nor the *Entertainments* seems to have been reprinted. One can conclude, then, that in England and among exiles, the reading public for the *Introduction* was far greater than for the other two works, and this follows naturally from the more specialized nature of their appeal.

It would be pleasant to be able to point to some English readers' reactions to St. Francis de Sales, in letters or elsewhere, and thus to trace some definite influence, but, except for the comments made by the translators themselves in their prefaces, nothing has been discovered. Nor is it possible to determine how great the reading public was as we do not know the size of the editions. It is in the nature of the times that exact information is almost impossible to come by. The translators, however, do give us some idea of what they thought of the original and what effect they hoped to produce, and undoubtedly did produce, by their labor of translation: a deepened inner life and a greater love of God. Spiritual guides were in short supply in recusant England; for isolated Catholics St. Francis de Sales became a living guide and friend, showing them "a safe and plain way to Christian perfection."[17] One can also state with certainty, from evidence submitted by one or two of the exiled communities that are still in existence here today, and in possession of a part at least of their original libraries, that the English translations of St. Francis de Sales were among their books.[18]

John Yaworth's translation of the *Introduction* is dedicated to the great-granddaughter of Sir Thomas More, Anne Roper, of Well

Hall, Eltham in South London where the fine house still stands, complete with its moat and drawbridge. In Stuart times this was an isolated country mansion. In the preface to his translation, Yaworth commends the book to her in the warmest terms:

> . . . it is like the philosopher's stone, containing in its small compass the seed of all metals, and changing baser metal into gold. There hath not come out any abridgment of devotion like this, containing so copiously in so few leaves, so plainly in sweet language, so profitably and aptly for the practice of all men, the rules and instruction of spiritual perfection, nor so pregnant in efficacy to convert the iron affection of our souls into the golden virtue of charity and true devotion . . . I read it carefully for the benefit of my own soul and translated it for the benefit of many souls in our poor distressed country, which more than any other country standeth in need of such good books for counter-poison against so many venomous writings, as worldly and fantastical heads do daily publish.

Although he offers the book to Anne Roper, the translator has chosen to address it to "Philotheus" and not to "Philothea," a form which remains until 1648 and also in the earlier Protestant editions. We are given a little more information about Yaworth in the 1648 preface by the priest of the English College in Paris:

> [The *Introduction*] . . . was formerly translated by a reverend person of our country; but he, in his great humility, exposing it to the review of others, it fell into the hands of some who, enlarging the author's style by so many unnecessary paraphrases, in diverse places confounded his sense. In this edition we hope to have remedied the inconvenience by following the true sense of the author, and his own expression, as near to the life as two languages will meet.

This version is, indeed, more taut and literal, but it has also lost some of its freshness and charm. Neither version was found to be

1. Statue of Notre Dame de Bonne Déliverance, the Black Virgin of Saint-Étienne-des-Grès, before which St. Francis de Sales, as a student in Paris, prayed the Memorare and was delivered from the temptation to despair. Presently this statue is in the convent of the Sisters of St. Thomas of Villanova, Neuilly-sur-Seine.

2. C. de Mallery, *St. Teresa of Ávila*, engraving from Francisco de Ribera, *La vie de la Mère Thérèse de Jésus* (Paris, 1602).

3. Portrait of Madame de Chantal in 1607. Monastère de la Visitation de Saint-Pierre-d'Albigny (Savoie).

4. Martin Baes, *St. Francis de Sales*, engraving from the first English translation of the *Treatise on the Love of God* (Douay, 1630). (courtesy DeSales Center for Lay Spirituality, Washington, D.C.)

5.   Portrait of Antonio Possevino, S.J.   6.   Portrait of Antoine Favre

7. Emblem 48 from Adrien Gambart, *La Vie Symbolique du bienheureux François de Sales, compris sous le voile de 52 Emblèmes* (Paris, 1664). See "Medieval Affinities," 164-65. (courtesy DeSales Resource Center, Stella Niagara, New York)

I, John Henry Newman, Superior of the Oratory of St Philip Neri, in Birmingham, certify that Alfred Paul Curtis, of Baltimore, in the United States of America, sometime a minister of the "Protestant Episcopal Church", was reconciled by me to the Church on the 18th April 1872, having previously made abjuration of his errors, and received conditional baptism, in my presence

John H Newman

The Oratory,
Birmingham,
10 May 1872

8. Certificate, in Cardinal Newman's hand, of Bishop Curtis' reception into the Catholic Church and conditional baptism (reproduced by permission of the Birmingham Oratory)

faithful enough by Richard Challoner who, after trying to revise, scrapped the older renderings entirely and began anew.

The Paris translators tell us about the purpose of their work and describe the nature of the book they were commending to their persecuted fellow countrymen:

> In affliction we commonly return to devotion; the former our friends in England have not wanted of late, and we hope they have had the latter, at least in their desires. This piece therefore will come very seasonably to them . . . . What is most precious to us we commonly carry about us: especially in a journey where the ways are dangerous, as well to secure it, as to take pleasure in often viewing it. This is a precious jewel; and our friends travel now in none of the securest countries: we shall therefore advise them to wear it about them and to view it frequently; not doubting but by God's grace the virtue of it will quickly pass through the eye to the heart where if it work the effect we desire, which is to inflame them with the love of God, we hope they will remember us in their devotions, who have remembered them in our labors, and shall never forget them at the holy altar.

The task which Miles Car set himself was an even greater labor. His translation of the *Treatise* (1630) has stood the test of time remarkably well, serving Dom Mackey as the basis of his translation more than two centuries later. As is evident from the number of copies of the book preserved in learned libraries of the time, for instance, in Cambridge colleges, this work of mystical theology reached a more specialized and therefore more restricted audience. This has called for a particular technique, for many of the scholastic terms used by St. Francis had as yet no accepted English equivalents, as Latin, "the language of the schools," had continued to be used by Protestant divines throughout the seventeenth century.[19] Miles Car says in his preface:

> Be pleased therefore to know that our author, being one of the greatest divines of his time in France, speaks now and then in school terms and formalities, which our

English will scarcely bear, especially in the highest and hardest matters of divinity, as predestination, the Trinity, etc. And again I desired that so worthy an author should rather be heard to speak in his own words than in my translation, esteeming faith not smoothness the grace thereof. Hence as far forth as the language would permit I have rendered his own words, turning "bonté" bounty, "amitié" friendship, though this sometimes had better been love . . . (but the learned reader will be indulgent with such words) . . . even though they have not yet gotten so free and known a course in our English tongue.

We know from at least one direct instance that Miles Car's faithful and skilled work had a not unimportant influence, notably on the spirituality of one of the great metaphysical poets: Richard Crashaw (1616-1650), of Pembroke College, Cambridge, and later a Fellow of Peterhouse. Expelled in 1644 as a royalist from Oxford, whither he had migrated, he found refuge in Paris, having by this time become a Catholic. There he was befriended in his poverty by Miles Car, who introduced him not only to the *Treatise*, but also to Queen Henrietta in exile. She helped him to ecclesiastical preferment and he died in Italy as a canon of Loretto. The effects of his reading of St. Francis de Sales are most plain to see in the poems he added in 1648 to his cycle, *Steps to the Temple* (1646). "He was imbued with the language of the *Treatise*—he caught its inflections and borrowed its metaphor,"[20] for instance, in one of his most famous poems on St. Teresa, "The Flaming Heart," and also in his adaptation of the "Stabat Mater" where he uses Francis' idea of the reciprocal nature of the wound of love:

> *Oh you, your own best darts*
> *Dear doleful hearts!*
> *Hail, and strike home and see*
> *That wounded bosoms their own weapons be!*[21]

a point that is elaborated in the *Treatise* in Book 6, chapters 13 and 14 ("Nothing so grievously wounds a loving heart as the sight of another wounded for love of its own heart"). It is typical of Crashaw that he singled out especially those elements of St. Francis' style and imagery that one would now describe as the most baroque, and that he tends to fasten on the curious analogies and images beloved by St. Francis, the fruit of his wide classical reading, but often remote to the modern consciousness. In spite of Crashaw's strange conceits and verbal obscurities, his poems have flashes of great lyrical beauty of a kind associated with St. Francis himself in some of the finest passages of the *Treatise* where the metaphysical thought turns, as it were, into the rhythm and music of poetry. Miles Car has faithfully preserved this effect in his rendering, whereas some modern translators, tending to see meaning as divorced from form, and not, as in the case of a true artist, as an indissoluble part of it, have wholly lost this effect, reducing St. Francis' prose to a uniform smoothness. Crashaw's chosen motto, prefixed to the *Steps to the Temple* was: "Live, Jesus, live, and let it be/My life to die for love of Thee!," the saint's own device. And his Protestant friend and fellow poet, Abraham Cowley, pays high tribute to this disciple of St. Francis de Sales who consumed himself "in a fire of love in his great Mistress' arms" at the shrine of Loretto, known and loved by him:

> *His faith, perhaps, in some nice tenets might*
> *Be wrong; his life I'm sure was in the right:*
> *And I, myself, a Catholic will be,*
> *So far at least, great Saint! to pray to thee!* [22]

The author of the last of the recusant translations of St. Francis, the *Delicious Entertainments of the Soul* (1632), was probably one of the gifted members of the More family; Our Lady of Cambrai, now Stanbrook Abbey, was founded by Crisacre More. The translation was undertaken, it is thought, at the suggestion of Fr. Augustine Baker, the community's confessor from 1624 to 1633. He greatly venerated St. Francis de Sales; and the idea of giving this young and eager group of English contemplatives some translation work to help absorb their energy and at the same time to form them spiritually would be a natural one. Certainly the nun who did the work gained greatly from it, even though she admits to not having "much skill in the

French," which is indeed evident in several places. But she has got to the heart of the matter, and what is more important, to the heart of St. Francis himself, whom she calls "one of the most clear, discreet, sweet and devout spirits of the age" whose advice in even the higher realms of the mystical life is suited "not only to religious persons, but also to the best seculars, especially of the devout sex." At the end of her preface she promises the reader the experience that evidently has been hers:

> For conclusion I dare boldly say, that whosoever will follow really and cordially the spirit of this author and book, he shall live in peace with God, with his neighbor and with himself. He shall taste upon earth how sweet God is in heaven, he shall lead a true evangelical or rather angelical life, he shall begin his heaven on earth and sail secure, immovable, quiet and content through all the changes and chances, storms and tempests of this wavering world, Jesus being his pilot, hope his anchor, faith his light, solitude his cabinet, prayer his provision, humility his haven, heaven his home. Farewell.

Apart from the moving testimonies of the translators and from the dated instance of Crashaw, one can point to some other channels of knowledge about St. Francis de Sales in England in the seventeenth century; but there again, anything as tangible as actual influence is hard to trace. One connection, that via the court, is at least sufficiently important to deserve further mention: England had two Catholic queens in this century, Henrietta Maria of France and Mary Beatrice of Modena. Henrietta and her large French suite lived here from 1625, the date of her marriage to Charles I, to 1644 when she was forced to flee to France. She returned for a time during the Restoration (1660) when her son Charles II was on the throne, and she died in 1669, sixteen years before the accession of her younger son, James II. The daughter of Henri IV and of Marie de Médicis, regent during Louis XIII's minority, Henrietta can be regarded as something of a personal link between Francis de Sales and England. Her most immediate connection with him was by way of her elder sister, Christine of Savoy, with whom she had close ties of friendship. Francis was

Christine's Grand Almoner,[23] he had gone to Paris in 1618 with the special aim of arranging her marriage to the Prince of Piedmont, he had blessed her marriage and traveled back through France in her suite the following year. She was in Lyons at the same time as her brother Louis XIII when Francis died in 1622; on Christmas Day, two days before his fatal attack, he left the Visitation and his gardener's cottage early to go to hear her confession and say the Mass at Dawn in her presence. Christine remained devoted to his memory always and was one of the greatest benefactors of his shrine and of the Visitation, especially the house in Turin; she did much to promote the cause of his canonization and lived to see it in 1665, as did her sister Henrietta Maria herself. The two sisters kept in touch by a lively and regular correspondence on family matters.

Their sister-in-law, Anne of Austria, had also known the saint, first meeting him at the time of Christine's marriage when Anne and her husband, Louis XIII, were both seventeen. Anne, childless for many years, attributed her safe delivery of an heir to the throne, Louis XIV, born in 1638, to the application of a relic of St. Francis. She held Madame de Chantal in high honor, and together with her two small children she knelt for her blessing when the foundress visited Paris for the last time, a few months before her death at the Moulins Visitation in 1641. This event shortly preceded Henrietta's arrival in Paris as a fugitive, when she put herself directly under the protection of her sister-in-law who was then regent.

Henrietta, too, visited Moulins on several occasions in order to see Madame de Montmorency, trained in the religious life by the foundress herself, and closely connected with court circles; like Henrietta, she had lost her royal husband by execution and in comparably tragic circumstances. The illustrious kinswomen wept and received consolation from each other's sympathy.[24] Henrietta herself founded a Visitation at Chaillot, then a village near Paris overlooking the Seine. There she lived in great simplicity, and by royal prerogative as a foundress, right inside the enclosure at times. She had wished to be buried at the monastery but only her heart in a silver urn found its last resting place there. Even her Protestant historian admits that "as such a retreat was necessary for her health and peace of mind, this foundation can scarcely be reckoned among her sins of bigotry, for it vexed no person's conscience, and provided for a community of harmless and charitable women who were at that time struggling with distress,"[25] a tribute, if a somewhat indirect one, to the order founded by Francis de Sales, who wanted his nuns to glory in their humility and their littleness in the eyes of the world.

Mrs. Strickland's accusation of bigotry was not entirely unfounded, for Henrietta's proselytism became rather insistent as she grew older; but the fact remains that her own devotion was true, and that Pope Urban VIII, who was her godfather and had given the dispensation allowing her to marry a Protestant, had at the same time laid upon her a serious obligation to help Catholics in England and promote the cause of the faith as best she could. Her presence in England was responsible for a secret clause in the marriage contract, seen and signed only by James I himself shortly before his death, but honored by his son, that active persecution of Catholics in England was to cease as far as possible. The political aim of her marriage to Charles I was in part to prepare the return of England to the Church, and Bossuet, who in his funeral oration on Henrietta preached at Chaillot where her heart in its urn was splendidly enthroned on a black draped bier beside a waxen effigy of the dead queen, said that by her own true view of kingship, and by her great personal charity to English Catholics, she had contributed much towards restoring a true view of religion in her adopted country. He considered her a "worthy and faithful disciple of the Order of Sainte-Marie," who preferred humility and the cross to worldly splendor and a throne.[26] Her attitude in marriage, motherhood, and as a widow was that of a woman who had been deeply influenced by the spirit and the teaching of the *Introduction*; her constant prayer in adversity was: "Lord God, Thou hast permitted it, therefore will I submit myself with all my strength." It is perhaps not too rash a speculation that this royal Philothea, both of whose sons became Catholics (James II in the prime of his life, Charles II on his deathbed) and who had such close links with the greatest French saint of her time, was in some sort an answer to his prayer for England and its royal house of Stuart. In a seventeenth-century painting at the church of Notre Dame de Bonne Nouvelle in Paris, this protection is graphically implied.

The saint and Queen Henrietta are shown together; he has the eldest boy, Charles, by the hand, the other child, James, is looking up at him confidingly while Henrietta herself is standing with her daughter. The Holy Spirit hovers in the background, where a vague landscape indicates England.

The same speculation may also extend to that other queen of England, the Italian Mary Beatrice of Modena, James II's second wife, who after her exile continued the close royal ties with the Chaillot Visitation, and herself lived and died there. Before her marriage she had tried her vocation at a Carmel and had then wanted to enter the Visitation founded by her mother in Modena: she married in obedience to reasons of state. Her arrival as a refugee at the French court in January, 1689, when she and James were forced to flee from England in dramatic circumstances was described in vivid letters of that date by St. Chantal's granddaughter, Madame de Sévigné. The queen's own letters and her relating of her adventures to her friend, Mère Françoise Angélique Priolo, at one time superior of Chaillot, formed the nucleus of a Visitation account of considerable historical value first used by Mrs. Strickland in her history.[27]

England is therefore indebted to the literary skill of a daughter of St. Francis de Sales for an important chapter in the history of the exiled Stuarts. For twelve years before she died in 1718, Mary Beatrice prayed nightly with the sisters at Chaillot for the conversion of England and the restoration of its rightful royal family. In 1690 a silver statue of James, the child heir to the English throne, whose birth had occasioned the deposition of his father in 1687, was sent by his parents to the tomb of Francis de Sales in the Visitation church at Annecy. In due course this votive effigy was joined by one of James' small sister, Louisa, pictured in her cradle, both children with their hands stretched out in a gesture of appeal to the saint, as if imploring his protection upon themselves and their country.[28] When it became clear to Mary Beatrice that there was little hope of another restoration and return to England for her son, and when both her husband and then Louisa died, she wrote to her Visitation friend: "According to the world our cause may be pronounced desperate, but according to God, we ought to believe ourselves happy, and bless and praise Him for having driven us to the wholesome necessity of putting our whole trust in Him alone."[29]

After her death at Chaillot she was buried there, and her own heart in its silver urn came to join those of Henrietta and of her husband and daughter. This cult of the heart as a symbol of the whole personality and particularly of its love, which throws a bridge, as it were, between earth and heaven, will remind us that the end of the seventeenth century saw the development in St. Francis de Sales' order of the devotion of the Sacred Heart of Jesus. From 1676 to 1678 St. Margaret Mary's Jesuit director, St. Claude La Colombière (1640-1682), was one of Queen Mary Beatrice's chaplains while she was in England. At her private chapel in St. James', founded by Henrietta, he preached the new devotion—the first of St. Margaret Mary's visions dates from 1673. He inspired the queen herself with interest in it and is said to have been personally responsible for many conversions among the English people who came to listen to his sermons. Greatly devoted to St. Francis de Sales and influenced by his spirituality, he was actively engaged in the project of the queen to found an English Visitation at Boulogne and corresponded with the superior at Paray-le-Monial on the subject.

If the plans for an English Visitation had got as far as having concrete backing at court and among recusant families, it is evident that knowledge of the founder and of his work must have been widespread and firmly established at the end of the century; and the new edition of the *Introduction* in 1686, the first Catholic one to be officially printed in England, is a further proof of this. But meanwhile his reputation had also increased in Anglican circles, as is clear from two separate Protestant adaptations of the book, one published in Ireland in 1673 by Henry Dodwell,[30] the other in London in 1701 by William Nicholls,[31] quite apart from the 1616 edition already mentioned, and the notorious edition of 1637.

In that year one of the Protestant editions that had already passed the state censorship of Archbishop Laud's chaplain, but into which "the same popish and unsound passages" had been reinserted (or so it was said) by the translator and printer, had the somewhat alarming distinction of being condemned to be burnt by a public proclamation of Charles I.[32] The book achieved this notoriety only because this particular reprint was used as a pawn in the strife between Laud and his Puritan opponents, who snatched at every opportunity of accusing him of popery; the proclamation was a political move to protect himself rather than an attack on Francis de Sales' book. Laud had painfully to explain the whole incident in the course of his trial later on when the *Introduction* that his chaplain was supposed to have licensed formed the subject of his enemies' fourth major charge against him. The crude censorship of fire was a popular way of dealing with condemned and dangerous books—Luther's works, for instance, were publicly burnt in St. Paul's Churchyard in 1521 while St. John Fisher preached to the assembled populace—but it seems a pity that a book as beloved by Anglicans and Catholics alike should, for reasons of state, have been singled out in this way. On 4 May 1637, the Archbishop wrote from Lambeth to the Vice Chancellor of the University of Oxford: "Eleven or twelve hundred were seized but it seems that 200 or 300 of the impression [of the *Introduction*] were seized before the official seizure. Now my desire is that if any copies of this translation be, or shall be, sent to Oxford, you would call them in, and take such order for suppressing them there as is here already taken."[33]

But holocausts such as this aside, devotional reading most certainly bridged the gap between the churches in England. Anglican literature of this kind was said by a contemporary to be "sober, just and godly," but to lack "comfort and sweetness." These last two qualities the *Introduction* supplied in full measure. Readers of every Christian allegiance were at heart agreed on this, and they saw the book as a most welcome focus of unity:

> And certainly it were much to the interest of Christendom that whatever controversies embroil the schools, all were exiled from books of devotion; . . . and it is more in the interest of *healing differences* to contrive devotional books which may be serviceable to all good Christians which otherwise would only advance a single party.

says Dodwell in his preface, while Nicholls in his translation of 1701 wrote as follows:

> Notwithstanding the great and deserved aversion which this nation has to popery, yet the books of their divines upon devotional and practical subjects have met with as

favorable a reception among us as if the authors had been of a better religion. . . . This Popish bishop is one of their best writers and does run not into the mystical stuff of Teresa, Blosius, Sancta Sophia, etc., though Sales has a little of it, too, which I have left out.

He evidently considered the instruction: "Place yourself in the presence of God," to be "mystical stuff," for this he has consistently omitted; and surely he can never have heard of the *Treatise*? But on the whole there is little interference with the text. Saints, except for "Mother Teresa," tend to be omitted, and so is anything connected with "images." Thus the advice to Philothea (and she turns from Philotheus into Philothea in Nicholls' version) to kiss her crucifix and hold it to her heart when she is overwhelmed by sadness is left out (Part 4, ch. 12); so is the chapter on the Mass (Part 2, ch. 14) and the one on the invocation of saints (Part 2, ch. 16). Vespers becomes evensong, and while the idea of confession as a sacrament is not retained, confession itself, the confessor, and especially the director, still feature throughout. On the whole we may say that the *Introduction* has fared better than the *Imitation* did in 1592 at the hands of Thomas Rogers; with straightforward honesty he stated the editorial principles which lasted on into the next century, but were implicit rather than explicit:

> In the doing whereof I have as little as might be varied from the truth of God, and nowhere from the sense, but where he himself hath varied from the truth of God, and I doubt not, would have redressed, had he lived in these days of light, as he did in the time of the most palpable blindness.[34]

Both the Anglican editors commend the style of the *Introduction*, Dodwell most ably and at great length, Nicholls briefly and more simply:

> There are many curious and uncommon reflections upon moral duties, and well chosen arguments for the practice of them. And the style withal is so familiar, easy and

inviting, that I am of opinion few people can begin to read the book without going through with it. For the natural and pretty similes and apposite examples, together with a peculiar tenderness and good humor in the expression are very entertaining . . . most good people will be the better for reading it.

Among the good people the better for reading it were Isaac Basire and his bride. He was an Anglican divine who was chaplain to the Bishop of Durham, and we are told that he sent a copy of the *Introduction* (we do not know which edition) to his future wife:

> A book . . . which next to God's own, my soul hath been much taken with. It was made by a French bishop, yet is the book free from popery (for I have read it aforehand for your soul's sake): only where you see a cross at the margin, there it may be mistaken by some; else all is safe.[35]

It would be interesting to know where the crosses were put and what precisely the term "popery" could have meant to Basire in this context. Bishop Thomas Ken of Bath (1637-1711), himself the author of a devotional handbook, *The Practice of Divine Love* (1685), had the works of Francis de Sales in his library, as well as those of Bellarmine, Bossuet, Fénelon (much beloved by Anglicans to this day), and even St. Edmund Campion.[36] William Sancroft (1617-1693), one time Master of Emmanuel College, Cambridge, and the Archbishop of Canterbury who crowned James II according to Anglican rites, was later imprisoned as a non-juror because he did not admit the validity of the king's deposal. Sancroft had several of the saint's works in French, English, and Latin in the library he left to his college. As this magnificent theological collection is still intact at Emmanuel, it gives a representative picture of the Catholic holdings of an Anglican of high culture and integrity.[37] Robert Nelson (1656-1715), a divine of Trinity College, Cambridge, who married a Catholic and who, although remaining Protestant, had staunch Jacobite sympathies, wrote a manual called *The Practice of True*

Devotion (1698) of which ten thousand copies were printed within four years, and which shows, both in its general disposition and in its detail, the influence of St. Francis de Sales.

These few names are given as an illustration of how pervasively the influence of this saint spread abroad in England outside his own communion. One name deserves more than a passing mention, that of Jeremy Taylor (1613-1667), who wrote a spiritual classic which occupies a similar position in the English cultural and devotional heritage as does the *Introduction* in France. Taylor's *Holy Living* (1649) and *Holy Dying* (1652) show throughout the imprint of a character and a personality similar, *mutatis mutandis,* to that of St. Francis; they resemble one another, too, in their wide humanist learning, their artistic skill as prose writers, and their insight into the human soul and psychology in general. Taylor's manual is distinguished, like the *Introduction,* for the orderly ease of disposition of the most varied material, the first sections of Taylor's book (holy living, the virtues, religion) corresponding roughly to the first three parts of the *Introduction;* it is true that St. Francis scores by his Latin brevity and greater powers of summary. Taylor does not address his Philothea personally, but he did write his book, in the first instance, for one particular person whose director he was: Lady Carberv at Golden Grove in Wales. After a brilliant university career—he was a son of the town of Cambridge and one of the most famous alumni of Caius College—he became a country parson, served King Charles I during the Civil War and was imprisoned, took up a dangerous ministry among Royalist Anglicans who lived in hiding during the Commonwealth, and finally went to Ireland where he was appointed Bishop of Down at the Restoration. He died not long after at the age of fifty-four.

Jeremy Taylor had the same care as St. Francis to reduce precepts to practice. Nothing is left in the air as vague theory, and Taylor supplies prayers as well as analysis and precept, though he also emphasized wordless prayer and aspirations. He follows up a nature image with the same joy as does St. Francis, not for its own sake, but so as to make his thought clear and concrete while at the same time engaging the reader's imagination and thus finally moving his will in the right direction:

For so have I seen a lark rising from his bed of grass, and soaring upwards, singing as he rises, and hopes to get to heaven and climb among the clouds; the poor bird was beaten back with the loud sighings of an eastern wind, and his motions made irregular and inconstant, descending more at every breath of the tempest than it could recover by the liberation and frequent weighing of his wings; till the little creature was forced to sit down and pant and stay till the storm was over; and then it made a prosperous flight, and did rise and sing as if it had heard music and motion from an angel, as he passed sometimes through the air, about his ministries here below: so is the prayer of a good man.[38]

Those who know and love St. Francis de Sales can here recognize the very accents of his tenderness, the same closeness to nature. Taylor's images are often strikingly original, as in St. Francis:

If you win secure a contented spirit, you must measure your desires by your fortune and condition . . . He that would shoot an arrow out of a plough, or hunt a hare with an elephant, is not unfortunate for missing the mark, or the prey.[39]

Ever and again he returns to his favorite, the bee, St. Francis' beloved *avette*:

Is that beast better that hath two or three mountains to gaze on, than a little bee that feeds on dew or manna, and lives upon what falls every morning from the store house of heaven, clouds and providence? Can a man quench his thirst better out of a river than a full urn, or drink better from the fountain when it is finely paved with marble, than when it swells over the green turf?[40]

The choice of imagery shows similarity of temperament and experience rather than influence, but there is one chapter more especially where Taylor is greatly indebted to Francis de Sales and actually mentions him as a source in a footnote: it is the heart of the book, the chapter on the Lord's supper (ch. 4, section 10), which corresponds to the *Introduction* (Part 2, ch. 21) almost throughout, but especially at the end:

> All Christian people must come. . . . They that have variety of secular employment must come; only they must leave their secular thoughts and affections behind them, and then come and converse with God. If any man be well grown in grace, he must needs come, because he is excellently disposed to so holy a feast; but he that is but in the infancy of piety had need to come so that he may grow in grace. The strong must come lest they become weak, and the weak that they may become strong. The sick must come to be cured, the healthful to be preserved. They that have leisure must come because they have no excuse; they that have no leisure must come . . . to sanctify their business . . . that as those creatures that live amongst the snows of the mountain turn white with their food and conversation with such perpetual whiteness, so our souls may be transformed into the similitude and union with Christ by our perpetual feeding on Him, and conversation, not only in His courts, but in His very heart and most secret affections and incomparable purities.[41]

These few examples can only give a slight idea of the affinity between Jeremy Taylor and Francis de Sales. How much the younger writer learned from the older, and how profoundly Francis penetrated into Anglican piety and practice through Taylor could best be appreciated if an edition of either work were furnished with a running commentary showing the correspondences. And this has, in fact, been done. The most scholarly of the newer English translations of the *Introduction*[42] is that of the Anglican priest, Thomas Barns, who illustrates his work on practically every page with a quotation from Taylor, or else one from St. Francis' *cher livre*, the *Spiritual Combat*, which Barns also translated (1909). This is a definite proof that through Jeremy Taylor the spirit of St. Francis reached the Anglican consciousness more widely, in a way, than through his works, with their more limited dissemination.

In this essay we have tried to show that, for England, St. Francis de Sales was the Doctor of Devotion long before the Church officially declared him to be so in 1877. He has always enjoyed a steady, even measure of popularity as the teacher who helps Christians, however much they may differ in their opinions, to attain individual holiness and therefore a closer union with one another. While it is unhistorical to look on St. Francis de Sales as a precursor of ecumenism as this term is now understood, it is certainly true that he prepared Christian concord and cooperation. Insofar as unity must spring, in the first instance, from charity, personal holiness, and the attempt to understand, that is, by emphasis on what unites rather than on what divides, St. Francis can be called one of the greatest ecumenical figures of the Counter Reformation, and the country in which his unifying influence has been most marked in this respect is England.

When the Archbishop of Canterbury left Rome after his meeting with Pope Paul VI, he went first of all to Geneva. On 24 March 1966, he preached on "The Recovery of Unity" at the Anglican church of the Holy Trinity before representatives of the other churches of the Canton and city of Geneva. This church is in a newer part of the town, separated by the narrow end of the lake from old Geneva. It is only a short distance, however, from St. Francis de Sales', and Calvin's, Cathedral of St. Peter on its fortified hill, of whose ancient ramparts and walls St. Francis once said, "Caritate quatiendi sunt muri Gebenensis," 'Charity is to break down the walls of Geneva, charity to invade the city, charity to recover it.'[43] In the course of his address Dr. Ramsey said:

> The recovery of unity, happening by God's grace at this time, means that the peace of Christ is reasserting itself, as Christians become more effectively bound to their Lord in humility and holiness, bound to one another in charity in an increasing number of ways, and bound within themselves as each Christian becomes less like legion and more like one man in himself . . . Jesus said: "'Peace be unto you.'" The true picture of the movement of Christian

unity is far more than the story of ecclesiastical events. It is the picture, known fully to God alone, of things happening in a thousand ways and in a thousand lives.[44]

From the time of the seventeenth century the influence of the written word and of the spirit of St. Francis de Sales has been felt in England "in a thousand ways and in a thousand lives." A former Bishop of Geneva, we may say, has helped to bring about a new set of conditions in which a modern Archbishop of Canterbury could, in the saint's own city, address an audience of this kind on the theme of unity.

NOTES

1. A. M. Ramsey, *The Gospel and the Catholic Church*, 2nd edition (London, 1956), 171.

2. David Mathew, *Catholicism in England*, 2nd edition (London, 1948), 261.

3. *Monumenta Pedagogica Societatis Jesu* quae priman rationem studiorum anno 1586 editam praecessere (Madrid, 1901).

4. Antoine Dufournet, *La jeunesse de Saint François de Sales* (Paris, 1942), 32. In 1583 Pope Gregory XIII had given permission for pictures of English martyrdoms to be painted on the walls of the English College at Rome. It is not impossible that Francis saw them on his visit to Rome in 1598.

5. *St. Francis de Sales: A Testimony by St. Chantal*, newly edited in translation with an introduction by Elisabeth Stopp (London/Hyattsville, 1967), 52 (hereafter *Testimony*).

6. Dom Jean de Saint François, *La vie du bien-heureux Messire François de Sales* (Paris, 1624), 221, and evidence of Michel Favre, First Canonisation Process, articles 17 and 27. The book in question is no longer in the Royal Library at Windsor and cannot be traced.

7. *Oeuvres*, 19:383, 17:325.

8. *Oeuvres*, 19:322.

9. *Testimony*, 133.

10. K. Lambley, *The French Language in England* (Manchester, 1920), 263ff.

11. *Introduction to a Devoute Life*, composed in Frenche by the R. Father in God Francis Sales, Bishop of Geneva and translated

into English by I. Y. (Douay, 1613). The orthography of the original texts has been maintained wherever possible in these notes.

12. *Introduction to a Devout Life, Leading the way to Eternitie.* Made by Francis de Salis, Bishop of Geneva. Christus Via, Veritas, Vita (London, 1616).

13. *A Treatise on the Love of God,* written by B. Francis de Sales, translated into English by Miles Car, 18th edition (Douay, 1630). Car's real name was Miles Pinkney (1599-1674); he was born at Durham, ordained at Douay, then for the rest of his life was chaplain to the English community of Canonesses of St. August in Paris, which owed its existence to his enterprise. He befriended Richard Crashaw, the poet, and he translated a work by Camus and also Bossuet's funeral oration on Henrietta Maria of England (1669). His translation of the *Treatise* preceded by twelve years the Italian one of 1642. The Latin one followed in 1643, Spanish in 1661, and German in 1668.

14. *Delicious Entertainments of the Soule,* written by the holy and most reverend Lord Francis de Sales, Bishop and Prince of Geneva, translated by a Dame of Our Ladies of Comfort in the Order of S. Benet in Cambray (Douay, 1632). A Latin translation appeared in 1648, Italian in 1652, Spanish in 1666, and German in 1667.

15. *A new edition of the Introduction to a Devout Life* of B. Francis de Sales, Bishop and Prince of Geneva, together with a summary of his life and a collection of his choicest maxims. Set forth by the English priests of Tourney College at Paris (Paris, 1648).

16. *An Introduction to a Devout Life,* written originally in French by S. Francis de Sales, Bishop and Prince of Geneva, faithfully rendered into English, with a summary of his life and a collection of his maxims (London, 1686). Printed by Henry Hills, Printer to the King's most excellent Majesty, for his Household and Chappel.

17. Roman Breviary, 2nd Nocturn, Lesson 6, for the Feast of St. Francis de Sales.

18. Thus the Franciscan monastery of Goodings, Newbury, Berks, which was founded in Brussels in 1621. This house also possesses a manuscript letter of St. Francis and one of St. Chantal, as well as relics of both saints, proving that their cult was considerable among the exiled English.

19. W. T. Costello, S.J., *The Scholastic Curriculum at Early Seventeenth-Century Cambridge* (Cambridge, Massachusetts, 1958)

20. A. F. Allison, "Crashaw and St. François de Sales," *Review of English Studies* 24 (1948): 302.

21. Richard Crashaw, "Sancta Maria Dolorum," *The Complete Works of Richard Crashaw*, Canon of Loretto, edited by W. J. Turnbull (London, 1858), 188.

22. Cowley, "On the death of Mr. Crashaw," as quoted by Turnbull, *op. cit.*, xvii.

23. Cf. his letter to her, 30 January 1620 (*Oeuvres*, 19:115).

24. Agnes Strickland, *Lives of the Queens of England*, 8 vols. (1840-48; London, 1864-65), 4:294.

25. Strickland, 302.

26. Bossuet, *Oraisons funèbres*, edited by Garnier (Paris, 1961), 139, 142.

27. Anonymous manuscript written by the Sisters of the Visitation of Chaillot, Bibliothèque Mazarine, Paris. A part of the MS was published as *Henriette de France à Chaillot* (Paris, 1890)

28. Roger Devos, "Le Pèlerinage Salésian," *Annesci* 10 (Annecy, 1963): 71.

29. Strickland, 5:392.

30. *An Introduction to a Devout Life*, containing especially a prudent method for spiritual closet-exercises, and remedies against

difficulties ordinarily occurring in the conduct of a pious life. Fitted for the use of Protestants. (Dublin, 1673). The name of the author does not appear, neither does that of the translator, but it is known to be the work of the Reverend Henry Dodwell (1641-1711), a professor at Oxford till he was deprived of office as a non-juror.

31. *An Introduction to a Devout Life* by Francis Sales, Bishop and Prince of Geneva. Translated and reformed from the errors of the Popish edition, to which is prefixed a discourse on the rise and progress of the spiritual books in the Romish Church, by Williams Nicholls, D.D., of Selsey, Sussex (London, 1701).

32. "A proclamation by the King for calling in a book entitled *An Introduction to a Devout Life* and that the same be publikely burnt," 14 May 1637. I have seen copies of this sheet at the British Library and at the Cambridge University Library. The text is given in Helen White, *English Devotional Literature 1600-1640* (Madison, 1931), 142. See also James Anson Farrer, *Books Condemned to be Burnt* (London, 1892), 88-89.

33. William Laud, *Works* (Oxford, 1853), 5:167. Of the copies that got away, only two are known to exist at the present day, both in the U.S.A., one at the Folger Shakespeare Library, Washington, D.C., the other at the Huntingdon Library, California.

34. White, 85.

35. White, 142.

36. F. P. Harton, "Spiritualité Anglicane," *Dictionnaire de Spiritualité*, vol. 1 (Paris, 1937). Campion's *Rationes decem* (1584) was used by St. Francis de Sales for his *Meditations on the Church*.

37. William Sancroft owned a French edition of the *Introduction* of 1638, the Latin one of 1616 (falsely attributed to Antonius de Sales and said to be very inaccurate), a French *Treatise* of 1618 and the very rare *Panthologie ou thrésor précieux de la Sante Croix* (Paris, 1613), *Defense of the Standard of the Holy Cross*.

There is an Italian life of the saint by Cristoforo Giarda, a Barnabite and Bishop of Castro (Rome, 1648). Sancroft also owned the *Bibliotheca Sacra* (1603-06) by Antonio Possevino, St. Francis' Jesuit director in Padua, and Bellarmine's *Controverses*. On Sancroft, see *Dictionary of National Biography*, vol. 50.

38. Jeremy Taylor, *XXV Sermons. Preached at Golden-Grove* (London, 1653), 59.

39. Jeremy Taylor, *Works*, edited by R. Heber, 12 vols. (London, 1847-52), 3:94.

40. Ibid.

41. Ibid., 220-221.

42. *Introduction to the Devout Life*. By St. Francis de Sales. Translated with notes and introduction by the Rev. Thomas Barns (London, 1906).

43. Address to the Canons of Geneva, December, 1593 (*Oeuvres*, 7:107).

44. The text of this sermon is to be found in *Theology*, 69, no. 552, London (June, 1966).

V

ST. FRANCIS DE SALES: ATTITUDES TO FRIENDSHIP

St. Francis de Sales is famous, one might say, notorious, for the important role that friendship played in his own life and in that of many privileged to call themselves his friends. This is clear, above all, from his letters: there are eleven volumes of them in the Annecy edition of his works with more than two thousand letters, though it is reckoned that there must have been many more than those which have survived.[1]

It is clear, too, from the testimonies of people in every walk of life who gave evidence at both the canonization inquiries, the first of which took place in his hometown in 1628 within six years of his death. It is clear from the moving and circumstantial accounts of his earliest biographers, men who were among his closest friends and also in immediate contact with Madame de Chantal who knew him better than anyone else. And although St. Francis did not join in the popular humanist pastime of writing a treatise—he did not even write a sermon or conference specifically on friendship as he never isolated this topic from the whole context of the love of God in his neighbor—he did, however, devote a few salient chapters to friendship in its social and moral context in the *Introduction to the Devout Life*, Part 3, chapters 17-22. *Amicitia*, like *caritas*, is also the constantly recurring, basic theme in the ten books of the *Treatise on the Love of God* (1616), planned and in part structured even before the *Introduction* (1609). Apart from his writing on the subject there are one or two outstanding friendships in his life with men of his own kind and caliber, for instance, that with his fellow-countryman, President Antoine Favre, and that with the Italian

Jesuit, Antonio Possevino. Here there is not only joint work and achievement is be taken into account, but in the case of Favre, there is also a two-way rather than a one-way correspondence of great interest. Looking at St. Francis' writing on the subject, then at the practice, will help to give a more rounded idea of what friendship meant to him.

On the whole, St. Francis' letters, lavish though they are in what may now seem exaggerated terms of endearment in the fashion of the age, are not always a true guide to his idea of friendship. To a large extent, except when he was writing on purely official business, his letters are letters of direction in answer to spiritual demands and difficulties. Even though this may well express true "friendship" on the part of a director, it inevitably loads a correspondence in a particular way, making it one-sided in most cases. The great majority of letters from his correspondents are, naturally enough, no longer extant; this means that the personality and attitudes of most of these correspondents have to be surmised from St. Francis' replies. But friendship is a matter of two-way communication, of to-and-fro interchange in a relationship which can never be rightly judged on one-sided evidence. This is a fact too often forgotten in the case of St. Francis de Sales, more particularly perhaps, in his deepest relationship, that with Madame de Chantal. All personal letters addressed to him in matters of direction were, as a matter of course, destroyed either by St. Francis himself or by his executors immediately after his death, except, that is, for those of Madame de Chantal written to him over a period of eighteen years from 1604 to 1622. A whole number of these, the majority, no doubt, of hundreds, he had himself prepared and annotated as what might be called spiritual copy, with a view to future publication in a context of his own. He was not only her director, friend and fellow founder, but he was a teacher by his very office as a bishop, and one, moreover, who was a dedicated writer, having spiritual responsibilities to a vast but invisible audience through the printed word.

The *Introduction to the Devout Life*, too, was based not only on the letters to his cousin, Madame de Charmoisy and others, but also, and quite importantly, on some of the earliest letters addressed to St. Chantal, that is, on those which had escaped an earlier holocaust of her letters. This was revealed to her director when he wrote to ask for their return for use in the second edition of his book in 1609.[2] It was one of the great differences between her and the bishop that, where he was a gradualist, a conserver, one who could let things be when it seemed best, she was given to swift, decisive, indeed violent action, of which the bonfire she made of all the letters returned to her in Annecy in 1623 after his death was a fitting symbol. Only very few, some forty in all, many just brief notes, somehow escaped the holocaust. She too it was who, together with St. Francis' brother and successor, prepared the first edition of his letters in 1626. And she it was who at that point resolutely cut out (this was revealed when the letters were compared with the surviving manuscripts for the Annecy edition) what might have been misunderstood as too personal in this unusual friendship; judging by some of the things that have subsequently been written about it, she may well have been perfectly right. "The world," she said in a letter of 1625, "cannot grasp the incomparble purity of this saint's love, her word here for the term "love" being the untranslatable *la dilection*, a love of willed choice, of election, St. Thomas Aquinas' *dilectio.* "This kind of thing," she goes on, "has to be taken very carefully,"—in her own brisk idiom: "Il faut avaler cela doucement."[3]

St. Francis' letters, "one-way" as they have come down to us, can never give a really adequate idea of what friendship meant to him personally. He rarely, except for the few chapters in the *Introduction*, isolated the topic of "friendship" from that of love of our fellows in general; all interchange and communion with true friends was, for him, basically "of the spirit." But the term "spiritual friendship" which he himself did use, though rarely, has gradually acquired a narrower, often sentimentalized meaning. In a world conditioned as now it is by a pervasive consciousness of sexuality and uninhibited emotionalism, a world of pansexualism, as it has been called, the term "spiritual friendship" has often, and quite imperceptibly, come to be understood as a mutual accord and interest in matters of religion to the exclusion of overexcited feelings and, of course, of sex. But St. Francis was bound to all who turned to him for advice and help quite simply in a relationship of love that was "spiritual" as a matter of course, a deep and steadfast love, surpassing all the present confused connotation of the words *ami*, "friend"; both the Latin and the Germanic root-words of this noun, *amare* and *frijon*, go back, quite simply, to the common derivation of them all, namely, "love." Except when St. Francis is analyzing friendship and love as conjugal virtues in the moral and social context, and for the benefit of lay-people, the bond of friendship, and this of course includes the friendship without which there can be no true marriage, is "in the spirit." This relationship must therefore be governed by the will and by reason, not primarily by the emotions, let alone the senses; this is precisely the fact that turns love, and the love that informs friendship, into something "spiritual." He is sternly explicit on what can transform a right and good friendship into a wrongheaded one.

His explanations in the *Introduction* to Philothea (the one who loves God) and in the *Treatise* to Théotime (the one who fears God) aim at showing to all who thirst for God that "the union which love longs for is one of the spirit," this being the heading of an important early chapter (Book 1, ch. 10) in the *Treatise*. A chapter near the end of the work sets out to explain "How holy charity makes us love our neighbor" (Book 10, ch. 11). This is what the love of friends meant to St. Francis and why he could, in all honesty, address his correspondents in terms of love and tenderness which may well now seem startling or merely sentimental. But this would be to ignore his understanding of the human psyche, his matter-of-course distinction between the will and the spirit, the emotions and the senses, and the different role they play in human relationships, in friendship, in marriage. St. Augustine, St. Bernard and St. Thomas Aquinas were his great mentors in such matters; he certainly also knew Cicero's dialogue on friendship, the *Laelius*, and even, it has been suggested, the christianized variant of this dialogue, the *De Spirituali Amicitia* by Aelred of Rievaulx. Such lore on *amicitia*, well known in the humanist tradition, was assimilated into St. Francis' own personal understanding of friendship.[4] Over and again St. Francis comes back to clear distinctions to make it evident that the love within friendship is not mere emotionalism, even though the love of God and of friends could, quite legitimately, be charged with strong feelings. But whereas emotion is almost wholly referable to oneself and essentially self-regarding, love is self-less, causing the lover to go and to remain outside self—*ex-stare*, standing outside and beyond self in the prime meaning of the word "ecstasy."

St. Francis' growing understanding of love as *caritas* and as *dilectio* which perfects love, led him to an ever deeper insight into the role of the "spirit" perfecting the human person by an ever growing love of God and of the neighbor in God, of the kind of love that informs true friendship. The story of this growing insight over the years is, in essence, what the *Treatise on the Love of God* is about. Love in the spirit was the foundation of his total spiritual program which is clearly stated in summary in the opening sentences of Book 10 of his *Treatise*:

> *Man is the perfection of the universe,*
> *the spirit perfects man.*
> *Love perfects the spirit*
> *and charity perfects love.*
> *That is why loving God*
> *is the aim, the perfection*
> *and the excellence of the universe.*

And this is the reason, the argument continues, why God actually *commands* us to love Him as we love ourselves, and also to love our neighbor as ourselves. This regards our will, not necessarily our feelings, which we cannot "command." By His grace and Our Lord's example "love in the spirit" is possible and within our reach; it can develop and grow, an ever more convincing dress rehearsal for heaven and for the perfect fulfillment of love. This, in simple summary, is what the *Treatise* sets out to describe. After outlining the history and the theory of the growth of divine love in the human heart as the Fathers and saints have described it (Books 1-4), he explains how self-surrendered prayer can help to make a reality of this ever growing love of God (Books 5-9) and how it works out in the humble, steadfast practice of everyday virtues among our neighbors whom we love in God and in the spirit. What the right love of friends meant to St. Francis can be fully understood only in the light of his teaching in this, his greatest work.

Though only published in 1616, the plan of the *Treatise* goes back to earlier years, most probably to St. Francis' meeting with Madame Acarie in Paris in 1602 when he read the first French translations of Teresa of Ávila. In *The Way of Perfection* she has some forthright things to say about the danger of self-deception in the matter of "spiritual" friendship, but she also writes with her usual vigor about the joy of true friendship "with those who are God's friends," "a very good way of 'having' God, as I have discovered by experience . . . under the Lord I owe it to such friends that I am not in hell" (ch. 7). St. Francis recommends the writings of Mother Teresa, as he calls her (she was not canonized until 1622, the year of his death), and it is clear that he had her ideas in mind when he wrote his own chapters on friendship in the first revised edition of the *Introduction*. She had a dispassionate insight into the dangers of that borderline territory where religion, emotionalism and desire coexist in a nebulous confusion. St. Francis, too, harbored no illusions about the danger of self-deception in that area. Like St. Teresa he stresses the importance of a right choice of friends, people who are "God's friends," intent on ever greater love of Him: we grow like what we love. This right choice is specially important for people in the world who can encourage and help one another as they walk along the "rough and slippery roads of the world"; they can cling to one another, giving support, counsel and stability when the going is hard. It is a relationship which needs "une grande communication" of things spiritual, even though friends must be on their guard that "false coinage" doesn't enter in along with "true gold." Friends of the right kind will soon learn and practice the distinction to be made between the words of Ecclesiasticus, "Those who fear God will also come by true friendship" (Eccl 4:17) and St. James' warning "nescitis quia amicitia hujus mundi inimica est Dei," 'don't you know that the friendship of this world is the enemy of God' (Jas 4:4, and *Introduction*, Part 3, ch. 22). Our Lord Himself and the apostles give us an example of true friendship "in the world" with quite an astonishing, and on the face of it, an unlikely selection of both men and women, all in their own way longing for God and loving Him. There are famous friendships among the Church Fathers, bishops among them, of course, and there are the saints, "simple and clear-eyed" in their loving friendships.

It is interesting to note that in the time between the first and the revised second edition of the *Introduction,* and with greater experience in directing souls, St. Francis saw the urgent need for ever greater clarity in guiding souls in this complex emotional area. The relevant chapters in the definitive edition as compared with the *editio princeps* have been considerably revised and expanded.[5] Clarity, as St. Francis saw it, was an essential prelude to moving the will towards right and often painfully hard decisions, the devil being an expert at clouding the judgment as a useful preliminary to a final assault on the will. The six chapters on friendship in the *Introduction* significantly enough follow on those dealing with chastity (Part 3, chs. 11 and 12) and with poverty (Part 3, chs. 14-16), both these topics considered in the context of life in the world. St. Francis prepares the minds of his readers for a true understanding of friendship by first of all stressing the need for people to control their greed for instant gratification; this he does by explaining the nature and the importance of poverty of spirit practiced amid "riches" in the area both of money and of sex. Throughout these chapters and in the follow-on analysis of friendship (Part 3, chs. 17-22), St. Francis is calmly explicit, he pulls no punches and leaves no room for illusion and easy compromise. It is amusing to compare the smoothly expurgated "revision" of St. Francis' book published a century later, a time already remote from the humanist straightforwardness of the late sixteenth and early seventeenth century.[6]

From accounts of his contemporaries it is clear that St. Francis himself had the joy of true friendship with many people; he had what the Italians call *attrativa,* the power to win hearts without trying; nor was he himself niggardly in his response to affection where he felt a true affinity of aims, of outlook. He had the generosity that could not only give, but could also accept, take and learn from his friends. One might single out, from among many, the joy and fulfillment he received in his friendship with two outstanding men of his time, both men older than himself who gave him support and stability by their encouragement, example and counsel, furthering him intellectually as well as spiritually. As it happens, both these friends had St. Anthony of Padua as their patron and model: it is perhaps too often forgotten that this saint did not only have a charismatic

Franciscan love of the poor and outcast, but was also a great preacher, a scholar and a Doctor of the Church.

The Italian Jesuit Antonio Possevino (1534-1611) was Francis de Sales' teacher, director and friend at the University of Padua during his three years of study there (1588-1591) for his double doctorate in law and in theology. Possevino, a native of Mantua, had been assigned to Padua in what was optimistically seen as retirement after a distinguished and adventurous career as a missionary, a teacher and writer, a diplomatic papal envoy to Sweden, Poland and especially to Russia where he attempted unity and reunion conversations at the court of Ivan the Terrible in 1581; he wrote an exciting account of this mission.[7] He had a great reputation, too, in France where he had worked in Jesuit houses in Lyon, Chambéry and at Avignon which he helped to establish. His understanding of the problems in the Geneva area gave him a particular interest in the gifted Savoyan student whose vocation he helped to clarify and affirm. Although he served as a model to St. Francis in matters both of the intellect and of the spirit—he was a man of hidden prayer—his friendship was also more immediately practical in that he nursed him through a spell of dangerous illness. All in all, he was something of a storybook Jesuit of the early vintage. From the letters, gifts of books and exchange of missionary and personal news that passed between them in later years, it is clear that they remained firm friends until Possevino's death in 1611. It was his work and example that made clear to St. Francis the absolute necessity of the written and printed word for winning souls in the Counter-Reformation context, and more especially for winning them back in view of the highly accomplished literary work of the Reformers. This helped St. Francis, not only through the hard missionary years in the Chablais and towards his own adventurous writing and publishing work there; it was a decisive influence on the future bishop of a divided and troubled diocese, a man who was also a director of souls and who had, even in his lifetime, a wide apostolate all over Europe through the printed word. Possevino himself remained a dedicated writer and editor throughout his life, his specialty being great handbooks and anthologies of important theological texts for the use of missionaries, theological "Readers' Digests," one might call them.[8] He gave constant and expert help to the great Counter-Reformation printing presses in

Venice, Rome and Lyon, he battled for the establishment of a polyglot press that would, for instance, include Cyrillic characters, not only Greek. He personally proofread all his own huge volumes, he saw them through the press and was in all these ways a model to St. Francis in his, not always easy dealings with printers and in the whole of the hidden, complex work that goes on before a writer's ideas and concerns are actually transformed into "a book." Possevino's help and friendship played a not insignificant part in the fact that St. Francis de Sales was named the Patron Saint of Writers and Journalists centuries later (1923).

Possevino, the apostle of the written and the printed word, also served as an inspiration, though rather differently, for the other Anthony in St. Francis' life, his fellow Savoyard, the lawyer Antoine Favre (1557-1624). Favre, ten years older than St. Francis, had been educated at the same Jesuit college of Clermont in Paris, and then also in Italy, at the University of Turin. He enjoyed the respect and confidence of the difficult Duke Charles Emmanuel of Savoy, he had the diplomatic skill to handle him and also to direct the legal thinking and the fraught legal problems of a dukedom divided by religious strife. He successfully pursued a legal and political career of great distinction, a career of the kind that St. Francis' father had always, but in vain, envisaged for his eldest son. Favre was in fact legal adviser to St. Francis' father, at whose rather pressing suggestion he had first contacted the son, not, perhaps, the most auspicious beginning for a good friendship. In succession Favre became the President of the Genevois Council of lawyers, then in 1610 the first President of the Senate of Savoy in Chambéry which later involved him in a term of office as civil and military governor of the whole duchy. When at that point he moved from Annecy he lent the house where he had lived with his large family to St. Francis and this became the "Palace" of the Prince Bishop of Geneva in exile. The following year, 1610, his eldest daughter, Marie-Jacqueline, entered St. Francis' new religious institute in Annecy, the Visitation. The links between the two friends could hardly have been closer, quite apart from the bond of affection in which each complemented the other in important ways. Furthermore, because quite a large correspondence between them has survived, it is possible to understand this friendship in a unique way.

There are first of all practical results of work and achievement in common: St. Francis wrote the first section, or "Premier Titre," of Favre's new code of Savoyan law, known as the *Codex Fabrianus* (1605), and together the two friends founded a scientific and literary academy in Annecy on the Italian model, the Académie Florimontane (1606), to encourage learning among local Catholics and in this way to help towards the Counter-Reformation drive for true scholarship among educated lay people.[9] What had been achieved in Geneva among the Calvinists was also to be done in Annecy. This was an intellectual and apostolic collaboration between friends: while Favre helped toward the administrative, social working out of their common enterprise, St. Francis supplied the theological knowledge and inspiration, but just as Favre was spiritually interested, St. Francis also had the legal point of view and knowledge. In other and more hidden ways the bishop meant much to his older friend. Favre was a happily married man with a large family—Claude Favre de Vaugelas, one of his sons who, as a boy, was allowed to listen in at some of the Academy sessions which took place in his father's house, later on became the author of the *Remarques sur la langue française* (1647) and one of the most influential members of the Académie Française founded by Richelieu in 1634. There was also another, more hidden bond between Antoine Favre and his friend. As a young man Favre had seriously considered a vocation to the priesthood; a certain nostalgia connected with this early dream never left him in spite of his brilliant public career and happy married state. It seems that his longing for a more complete religious commitment found a kind of fulfillment in the—quite unexpected—vocation and dedicated contemplative life of his daughter, Marie-Jacqueline, who made her decision after refusing an offer of marriage from St. Francis' younger brother. She became Madame de Chantal's closest friend and helper, a good superior in her turn, who remained in constant touch with the guide and director who had known her since childhood. This meant much to her father, as did his friendship with St. Francis, a like-minded younger man who had managed to put across a vocation to the priesthood in the face of family opposition and a resulting conflict in his own conscience.

The friends also collaborated as authors and writers. Favre had ambitions to be a poet, that is, something more than the ready versifier he in fact was. He published two sonnet sequences, or "Centuries" as they were termed, but as he was short on ideas for subject matter, he took the themes from his friend's sermons and dedicated the poems to him in gratitude, to St. Francis who, though no poet, became a great spiritual writer. A more impressive literary monument to this friendship than Favre's rhymes was St. Francis' contribution to Favre's *Codex Fabrianus* of 1605.[10] At Favre's request St. Francis wrote the introduction to the whole Codex, *De Summa Trinitate et Fide Catholica*. The work was jointly planned, then edited by Favre who made some emendations in the later pages. In his own preface to the Codex he added words of warm thanks and praise about the author of the First Title who had by then—the work was begun in the Chablais days—been raised to the bishopric of the whole region of Geneva. Favre's object in composing a new Codex for Savoy was not only to provide an up-to-date work of reference in a duchy of divided religious allegiance and long devastated by civil war; he had an apostolic intention. Lawyers and magistrates were influential people with whom Favre worked closely in the Genevois region, and many of them were, of course, Calvinists. The First Title, as an essential basis, was designed to show that the whole fabric of the Roman legal system as it had come down through the centuries from the *Codex Justinianus* (A.D. 529), and which had formed the background of legal studies for both Favre and St. Francis in Italy, depended on a right understanding of the relative position of the civil and the ecclesiastical authority, of state and church. The new Codex for the Catholic dukedom of Savoy was printed in France, in Lyons, there being no adequate press in the region except at Geneva. It bore the approbation and imprimatur of three Catholic doctors of divinity of whom Jean Déage, St. Francis' tutor and lifelong friend, was one.

The First Title of the Codex is a closely argued, well-documented piece of exemplary Latin, an analysis of relevant texts, more especially those by Luther and Calvin. Throughout, St. Francis stresses the fact that he has had official permission to read and to quote from the Reformers' texts, an important piece of information for Catholic lawyers and magistrates using the Codex, for they had never, or only rarely, had occasion to read works which were on the Index. He also makes it clear that he is arguing his case in his capacity as a jurist and a doctor of law, and not only, or even primarily, as a theologian; the Reformers are to be proved wrong on legal grounds, on their defiance of accepted common law, on their consistent mode of negation and denial as also on their own contradiction of one another. Negative inner contradictions of this kind can never lead, so he argues, to what is whole, positive and creative, or to anything remotely resembling the seamless truth they are trying to destroy. St. Francis' paragraphs begin with the words "negando affirmant," 'they affirm by denying,' and his argument ends with the terse conclusion, "credendo non credunt," 'they believe by not believing.' Sometimes he just quotes the Reformers' mutual contradictions verbatim and without further commentary, simply allowing these writers to tie themselves up in knots, and leaving it at that. Whereas Favre's tone tends to be fierce and trenchant (the Annecy editors have put brackets round his emendations to the original text as submitted by St. Francis), the latter writes more in sorrow than in anger. His courteous and moderate tone was his own particular contribution to a common apostolic effort of friendship. The First Article ends on a note of grief and in an appeal to the lawyers using the new Codex, men often personally known as *amicissimi*, "dear friends," to the writer. He begs them to think earnestly about the legality of their position in the light of the arguments put forward for their consideration. The final sentence is a plea *in caritate Dei* to forgive him if he has said anything that may sound too harsh, or of a kind to offend them as "adversaries" or "heretics," whereas his appeal is to them as "friends."[11]

The Latin of the Codex is necessarily official and impersonal; this cannot be said of the style of the Latin correspondence between Favre and St. Francis carried on in the early years of their friendship, from the months before St. Francis' ordination in December 1593, right through his missionary years in the Chablais and until he too moved to Annecy in the early years of the new century. The initiative for this correspondence came from Favre. The reason why it has come down to us at all, in the shape of some forty letters from St. Francis, and thirty-four from Antoine Favre, is that both writers made drafts of their letters which they kept, so to speak, as their own carbon copy. These drafts were later copied for the canonization inquiries. Some of the original drafts, and even a few fair copies, still exist in manuscript in the Annecy Visitation archives and elsewhere. It is revealing for the nature of this correspondence in humanist style that there should have been these drafts by men who led busy lives. They were writing for the pleasure of composition, to keep their Latin style in good trim with all its ingenious twists and turns, and with the overriding object of giving mutual delight among friends each of whom knew and appreciated exactly what the other was doing. Compliments on good style and happy formulations flowed freely between them, however serious the actual news and matter that was being discussed. Both friends make use of the traditional hyperboles and superlatives of regard and affection, but at the same time show real joy in the friendship of an *alter ego* with whom hopes and fears, failure and achievement, important and unimportant thoughts, or just sheer high-spirited fun and wordplay could be freely shared. This kind of joy in *bien trouvé* turns of Latin phrase and neat allusion, even in punning as a nice display of wit, still survives even in twentieth-century England as a live form of art at both the ancient universities when honorary doctorates are conferred. The University Orator then delivers a number of Latin speeches he has composed to sum up the career of the person being honored, be it a great scientist or theologian, a poet or a musician, Mother Teresa of Calcutta or the King and Queen of Spain. The orations are then printed in the current *University Reporter*—with an English translation for the benefit of those senior members of the university whose Latin has perhaps grown rusty, or, towards the end of the century, does not exist at all.[12]

Such letters, then, as exchanged by Favre and St. Francis, were a service of friendship. Giving delight by a carefully composed piece of writing was a heritage of classical culture, an important aspect, too, of medieval and monastic letter writing, taken over by the humanists and taught in their schools and colleges, such as Clermont in Paris, or Colet's St. Paul's in London. One only has to think of the splendid letters of, for instance,

Erasmus and Thomas More on the pattern of Cicero and in the ancient Christian tradition of the Fathers, so often quoted and recommended in St. Francis' own letters later on. The humanist letter had fixed rhetorical patterns and set forms of address which had to be learnt and observed. Antonio Possevino, for instance, in his *Bibliotheca Selecta*—St. Francis owned and greatly valued his own copy of the work—had a section on the nature and the history of letters as a set literary form, together with instructions on how best to go about their composition.

Using Latin for the correspondence between St. Francis and Favre was a pleasant humanist exercise, but there was also a more sinister reason: post from the Chablais was not secure so that news of progress, comments on the situation, were naturally more arcane and safer in Latin than in French. Important news was put across among general reflections and quotations from Aristotle, Cicero, Virgil, Horace, St. Thomas and the Church Fathers, or else suitably mournful wisdom from Job, Jeremiah and the Psalms, all of which seemed harmless enough on the face of it. St. Francis unburdens his heart, tells of his weariness and discouragement, his sense of the failure of his ministry, but there is always firm hope and trust in God, in prayer and penance as the great answer to all faintheartedness. When things seem unbearably hard, St. Francis pictures his friend as comfortingly close to him and then light breaks on the gloom spread abroad by the Prince of Darkness. This he says in a letter written from the fortress of Les Allinges, the rocky fortified stronghold overlooking the Lake of Geneva—it was there he had to live in the early months of his mission.[13] At this difficult time, St. Francis founded a brotherhood of the Penitents of the Holy Cross, and Favre organized a branch of it in Chambéry. Every holy image, but particularly the crucifix, was a special focus of attack on the part of the Reformers; as a counterattack, St. Francis and Favre each led their band of cross-bearing penitents barefoot along rocky ways to meet for an open-air service at a halfway point. All this was arranged in their Latin letters. At this time St. Francis also wrote a treatise in French for the benefit of his learned opponents, explaining and defending the use of this image, *Défense de l'Estendart de la Sainte Croix*, not published till 1600. This was a subject of joint interest and effort on the part of the two friends. This work, dedicated to the Duke of Savoy, had a long preface addressed to the Penitents of the Brotherhood, of whom Antoine Favre was, of course, one. A copy of the work was sent to Antonio Possevino, then in Venice, by a reliable special messenger who was, in fact, a Chablais convert of St. Francis'. Possevino highly commended the work and planned to include the whole of it in a second edition of one of his great compendiums.[14]

Favre's letters to his friend, *amicissimas litteras*, as St Francis calls them, are full of warm encouragement and expert advice, his particular contribution; St. Francis for his part always offers his Mass *tuo meoque nomine*, as he tells his friend, having a vivid sense of his presence close beside him at the altar. In reply to Antoine Favre's sons—the nine-year-old Claude had written him a letter in accurate Latin—he tells them that if they are "good apprentices," they will, in the course of time, emerge as *fabri nobilissimi* from their father's "workshop"—a pun on the Latin *faber*, that is, "artisan" or "workman," the French name, Favre, being as common a surname in that region as our "Carpenter." And in the meanwhile, how right Claude and his brothers are to follow the chief Faber's excellent example in writing so lovingly, *tam amanter*, to their father's friend.[15]

Their correspondence apart, the friends often undertook travel and work assignments together; thus in July 1597 they visited Théodore de Bèze in Geneva for theological conversations suggested by the Vatican. The talks were not a success in that de Bèze, naturally enough, did not change his mind; but the way the two Catholics conducted the conversation, carefully complementing one another in this difficult and delicate mission, seems to have been a great help to them both while it left de Bèze, an old man by then, with the conviction that civilized talk on religious differences was at least possible, even with two ardent young papists.[16] Together, the friends also took time off, walking up into the mountains to the remote Cistercian monastery of Hautecombe and having a brief interlude of the contemplative life as guests of the monks. Often, too, Favre was the guest of the de Sales family at their second home by Lake Annecy, the Chateau de la Thuille, or the *Casa Tulliana*, as Favre called it. They were in Paris together on "Provost" Francis' first official visit there in 1602, and this was preceded by a joint visit to Rome (1598-99) where they shared lodgings, visited the churches and made the local pilgrimages together, discussing the official work to which each was assigned, St. Francis on behalf of his bishop, Favre for Duke Charles Emmanuel. When, in 1602, his friend was consecrated bishop at Thorens, his mountain home village, Favre was there, to make up for the fact that he had been unable to get to the ordination there nine years earlier on. One of St. Francis' most moving letters, in which he tells his friend about his state of mind at the prospect of ordination and of this total commitment to God, dates from this time, the knowledge that such emotions and ideas can be shared and completely understood by the other, being, for him, for them both, one of the greatest joys of friendship.[17]

The exchange of letters virtually came to an end when St. Francis, as bishop, came to live in Annecy in a street close to Favre and his family, when they worked together in their jointly founded Academy, presiding at the various sessions until Favre was again promoted and had to move to nearby Chambéry. He outlived his younger friend by only just over a year—he died in February 1624, and St. Francis at the end of December 1622. He was, however, as one might say, invisibly present at both the canonization processes for St. Francis, in Annecy in 1628 and in Paris thirty years later, when all their letters formed part of the evidence put forward, and when Antoine's son, Claude Favre de Vaugelas, attended the Paris Process in person. The relationship between Favre and St. Francis fulfilled what he had described in the *Introduction* as an ideal friendship in the world: two people going through life in a shared communication of all that is good and holy, giving one another courage and hope, urged on by the same spirit, working towards the same end in shared effort, shared affection. Truly, as St. Francis says as he concludes these chapters of his book, St. Thomas Aquinas—like any good philosopher—is right when he says that *amicitia* is a virtue, quite simply because a good and right friendship is, in fact, love, *caritas*.

NOTES

1. See *Oeuvres*, vols. 11-21 (*Lettres*). Also see François de Sales, *Correspondance: Les lettres d'amitié spirituelle*, edited and annotated by André Ravier, S.J. (Tours, 1980), and St. Francis de Sales, *Selected Letters*, translated with an introduction by Elisabeth Stopp (London/New York, 1960).

2. Letter of mid-February 1609 (*Oeuvres*, 14:131).

3. *Sainte Jeanne-Françoise Frémyot de Chantal: Sa vie et ses oeuvres*, 8 vols. (Paris, 1874-90), 5:538, in a letter of 1625. The letters of St. Chantal, two thousand in all, are contained in vols. 4-8 of this edition. A critical edition of the letters is now in progress at Annecy: Sainte Jeanne de Chantal, *Correspondance. Tome 1, 1605-1621*, edited and annotated by Sr. Marie-Patricia Burns, V.H.M. (Paris, 1986). This fine edition should be consulted for the most reliable version of St. Chantal's letters to St. Francis. The most perceptive analysis of the friendship between the two saints is still that of *Michael Müller, Die Freundschaft des hl. Franz von Sales mit der hl. Johanna Franziska von Chantal*, Eine moral-theologisch-historische Studie (Munich, 1924; 2nd edition 1937, French translation 1936). A more recent study is that by Wendy M. Wright, *Bond of Perfection: Jeanne de Chantal and François de Sales* (New York, 1985). See too the present writer's *Madame de Chantal. Portrait of a Saint* (London, 1962, and Westminster, Maryland, 1963).

4. See Ruth Murphy, *Saint François de Sales et la civilité chrétienne* (Paris, 1964), 159-170, "L'Amitié vraie," and throughout for the relevant moral and social background of the age in France. See also G. Vansteenberghe, "L'Amitié," *Dictionnaire de Spiritualité*, vol. 1 (Paris, 1937), 500-529, with a full bibliography.

5. See *Oeuvres*, vol. 3, where the whole of the *editio princeps* of 1609 appears after the text of the revised *Introduction* as it has come down to us, and there are indices of the two editions comparing their structure. There are only two chapters on friendship in the first edition. Also see the preface and notes to the

Introduction in the Bibliothèque de la Pléiade edition of Saint François de Sales, *Oeuvres*, edited by André Ravier, S.J., in collaboration with Roger Devos (Paris, 1969). It may be noted in passing that the authoress of *La Princesse de Clèves* (1678), the most famous seventeenth-century novel about conjugal faithfulness and friendship, was a great reader of the *Introduction* and a close friend of St. Chantal's granddaughter, Madame de Sévigné.

6. *Introduction a la vie dévote de Saint François de Sales, Évêque et Prince de Genève*, Fondateur de l'Ordre de la Visitation de Sainte Marie. Edition nouvelle, Revue par le R.P.J. Brignon de la Compagnie de Jésus. A Brusselle, MDCCIX. My copy has the bookplate and arms of an English Recusant, Jemima Duchess of Kent. MDCCX, and also that of Thomas Philip, Earl de Grey, with his motto: FOY EST TOUT.

7. Antonio Possevino Soc. Jes. *Moscovia et alia opera, de statu huius seculi - adversus Catholicae Ecclesiae hostes.* In Officina Birkmannica, 1587. There is a facsimile reprint of this work (Gregg International Publishing Ltd., Farnborough, Hants. G.B., 1970).

8. *Bibliotheca Selecta qua agitur de ratione studiarum in Historia, in Disciplinis, in salute omnium procuranda.* Rome 1593. The Cambridge University Library has this first edition and also one of 1607, while Emmanuel College has the editions of 1597 and 1603 in the Sancroft Library. Sancroft, Archbishop of Canterbury, and later, Master of Emmanuel College, left his books to the College. The *Bibliotheca Selecta* and other compendia by Possevino were to be found in most learned libraries of the seventeenth century.

9. For the statutes of the Académie Florimontane, 1606, see *Oeuvres*, 24:242ff, and Frances A. Yates, *The French Academies of the Sixteenth Century* (London, 1947), 282-284.

10. *Codex Fabrianus definitionum forensium et rerum in sacro Sabaudiae Senatu tractatarum* (Lyons, 1606, and five later editions). The Latin text of the First Title, with a French translation, is to be found in *Oeuvres*, 23:67-241.

11. *Oeuvres*, 23:241

12. The Annecy editors have given only the Latin text for Favre's letters, (*Oeuvres*, 11:371-428), but have supplied a French translation for St. Francis' letters. This has been taken over by A. Ravier (see note 1 above) in his selection under the heading, "Une amitié exemplaire," 3-52. See also his entry under "Amitié" in his index entitled "Spiritualité de St. François de Sales d'après sa correspondance," 771-74. Ravier gives both friends, but especially Francis, bad marks for what he calls "preciocité." This does little justice to the style of letters written in the set humanist mode which cannot be fairly judged in translation. Only a few of the later letters in the correspondence were written in French.

13. Letter of October 1594 (*Oeuvres*, 11:90).

14. For the letters which passed between the friends on this occasion, and for the exchange of gifts of their works, see *Oeuvres*, 13:105-110, 399-402. In 1595 Possevino had sent the *Moscovia* (see note 7 above) and a small pocketbook anthology of songs and poems introduced by an essay on poetry. This was an extract from the *Bibliotheca Selecta*, entitled *Tractatio de Poesie et Pictura ethnica* (Lyon, 1593), and was designed to give missionaries an idea of the importance of poetry and song in their work. This attractive book delighted Francis as "a true portrait of his friend's mind and spirit." The Cambridge University Library has a 1593 edition of the book.

15. Letter of 15 August 1594 (*Oeuvres*, 11:79-80).

16. Théodore de Bèze (1519-1605), the humanist writer and theologian who succeeded Calvin as head of the Church of Geneva, is well remembered at the Cambridge University Library by a fine portrait and by his gift to the library of one of the oldest manuscripts of the Gospels and Acts, now known as the *Codex Beziana*. The MS had come from a Benedictine monastery in the south of France and was officially presented to de Bèze during the French Civil Wars. His object in passing it on to Cambridge was to establish good relations with Queen Elizabeth and with the Anglican Reformers, an object in which he failed.

17. Letter of 15 December 1593 (*Oeuvres*, 11:37-40); Antoine Favre's heartening and detailed reply dates from 20 December (*Oeuvres*, 11:379-382).

VI

The First Biography (1624)

Francis de Sales died on 28 December 1622, and by the summer of 1624 two *vitae* of him had already appeared, the first published in Paris by Jean Goulu, in religion Dom Jean de Saint François, Superior General of the Feuillants;[1] the other in Lyons by Messire de Longueterre, an ecclesiastic belonging to Francis de Sales' household at Annecy.[2] The following year the Franciscan Minim, Louis de la Rivière, who had preached the Lenten sermons at Annecy in 1616 and also knew Francis well, published his account,[3] and then in 1628 the Provincial of the Capuchins in Savoy, Philibert de Bonneville, followed with yet another life. He had, in a sense, been first in the field, since it was he who had preached at the saint's funeral; his book was an expanded version of the already published oration.[4]

These four works were written in more or less close collaboration with Francis' immediate circle, especially with his brothers, Jean and Louis, the first being his successor as Bishop of Geneva, the second the heir to the family title of the influential de Sales family. It was Jean-Pierre Camus, bishop of the neighboring diocese of Belley, who supplied de Longueterre with notes and information. But the most important person, the moving spirit behind the endeavor to have Francis' life accurately described with a view to early canonization, was Jeanne Françoise de Chantal. She was his closest disciple and together with her he had founded the Order of the Visitation at Annecy in 1610. It was she who now gathered together most of the material for the *vitae*, either in *mémoires* she herself had written, or had encouraged others to write. Her letters of the years 1623 and 1624 are full of references to this activity. She was tireless in answering questions, lending letters and other manuscripts, and in stimulating properly qualified people to edit the correspondence and the sermons of Francis de Sales. It was she too who helped to set in motion, from within her monastery enclosure, the complicated procedure for canonization inquiries. During the first local process, begun at Annecy in 1628, she was herself the chief witness and gave evidence about her director in a testimony of great penetration and beauty.[5] She based her deposition on the *mémoires* she had recorded five years earlier. These have now been lost, but it is known that she sent them to Jean Goulu, and possibly to him alone among the early biographers. He was therefore from the very beginning in a position of special advantage, and also of trust.

In the final article of this official deposition she cites the first four *vitae*, placing that of Jean Goulu at the head of the list, but giving them all sanction and status as accurate and trustworthy accounts. But even after the official inquiries, she, and all at Annecy who were pursuing the cause, felt that the life in which the year-by-year chronology was given in detail had yet to be written. On the whole, the earlier authors, all of them close to their subject in age and time, had tended to take chronology for granted and concentrate more on the saint's personality and spirit. Louis de Sales' son, Charles-Auguste, provost of the Geneva chapter, and about twenty-six at the time, was commissioned to write an accurate and comprehensive life of his uncle which could be sent as evidence to Rome. The book appeared simultaneously in Latin and French in 1634.[6]

Charles-Auguste had access to all the family papers, he could discuss every point with his relatives, and as cathedral provost, he could work through the episcopal archives and records. Most important of all, he could talk to Madame de Chantal and even read out his work to her in the Visitation parlor; he consulted her at every turn, and when the time came, she and the sisters helped with the proofs. Subsequent research has shown that, even so, quite a number of errors about the time sequence remained, but the only important matter of substance missing in the book is everything connected with the Visitation and Madame de Chantal herself. Her discretion and reticence would allow of nothing else. Although Charles-Auguste mentions the titles of the earlier biographies in his impressive list of sources, the only one he singles out for special comment and praise right at the beginning is that of Jean Goulu. He also pays him the compliment of borrowing from him many phrases and striking formulations unchanged, especially anything connected with Francis' writings, or any incident that needed concentrated or epigrammatic telling. One has the impression that he wrote with Jean Goulu's book propped open in front of him. This is worth stressing, for whereas Goulu's work has now been forgotten, perhaps largely because it is so rare of access, Charles-Auguste's has remained the standard early biography even though treated with some reservations. But he owed much to the older and infinitely more skilled writer. The nephew's book remains what it was intended to be—a valuable chronicle and source book, the work of a painstaking, earnest young man who was making the best of a difficult job and had neither the wish nor the power to select material and give his book true literary shape.

Together with the six-volume work of conversations and anecdotes by Francis de Sales' Boswell, Jean-Pierre Camus,[7] the *vitae* so far mentioned make up the complete body of the printed source material for the saint's life. Of these, only Goulu, Camus, and Charles-Auguste have been reprinted in modern times. No one has survived as a literary work in its own right, and it is true that the *Life* by Jean Goulu is the only one for which a claim of this kind might possibly be made. De Longueterre padded his discursive book with endless and inapposite classical parallels and allusions. De la Rivière, a prolific writer, sermonizer and near-mystic of the kind beloved by Bremond, makes the events of his subject's life the occasion for long disquisitions on the virtues and on prayer. Philibert de Bonneville chose to keep tenaciously to the plan of his funeral oration which was not based on a time sequence but on an anagram of the saint's name: "ce soleil sans fard"; the text was Ecclesiasticus 50: "Comme le soleil reluisant, de mesme cestuy-cy a reluy au temple de Dieu." De Bonneville, too, has long rambling interpolations on prayer and on earlier saints. There are interesting personal impressions in all these accounts, and they have much individual charm and great sincerity, but on the whole the impression left by them is one of confusion and lack of discipline in the face of a mass of material. There is, too, the natural desire to edify at all costs and point morals at every turn. It would be unrealistic to count this as a fault for it is wholly in keeping with the genre of the *vita* of a saint and it has come down from the earliest times of the Church.

The *vita* was a conventualized form with a single devotional object and an extremely limited range, and it must be counted on the credit side of the books mentioned that they were at least completely free from the legendary element which so easily and quite unconsciously crept into them. The scholarly investigation of the lives of saints was only then beginning; the first Bollandist publication dates from 1612. J. P. Giussano's life of St. Charles Borromeo, acknowledged as a model of sober and accurate chronicling, also dates from Francis de Sales' own lifetime (1610). Though there had been many straightforward and reliable *vitae*, and even some masterpieces in this genre before the Counter Reformation, they were perhaps rather the exception, and it was only on their general qualities of accuracy and soberness that the *vitae* of the later sixteenth-century saints—Ignatius Loyola, Teresa of Ávila, Francis Xavier, and the Jesuit missionaries in the East— showed any considerable improvement. Erasmus' brief lives of, among others, More and Colet, and also the attractive Tudor biographies of More by Roper and Harpsfield, form notable exceptions here and are in any case somewhat apart from the mainstream.[8] Erasmus, for instance, does not set out to write a life; he tends to give selected and subtle traits of character rather than events in chronological sequence. On the whole, the form was too limited and too exclusively concentrated on its single biographical purpose to allow of anything really creative in the reconstruction of the saint's life and character. Certainly, with one exception, the authors of the early lives of Francis de Sales hardly suspected the creative possibilities inherent in this form; in fact, they expressly, if not always sincerely, disclaim literary polish as something not really quite proper and correct under the circumstances.

It is, then, with rather a pleasant shock of surprise that one finds Jean Goulu beginning his *Vita* with some reflections on the nature of religious biography and its peculiar difficulties. In trying to describe the beauty of holiness, the writer is faced, he says, with the same problem that confronts an artist about to paint a face where beauty lies in a perfect harmony of features and their subtle interrelationship. How much easier when there is some element of disharmony, some scar or "une partie hors oeuvre," rather than in a case where the subject's virtue, grace, and interior beauty are harmoniously balanced in a perfectly ordered relationship. Writing about someone like St. Augustine, he says, would have been much simpler; there was that spectacular debauchery of his younger years, the strong conflict within him, his broken resolutions, his dramatic conversion. In the present case there is nothing of all this, and the author fears the story will appear rather more dry in consequence; indeed, the reader may even be less appreciative of Francis' perfection because of this lack of contrast.

From the outset these reflections strike a very different note from the contemporary hagiographers who were unreflectingly identified with their task and had little detached artistic awareness of the problems inherent in the form they were using. Where for others, the conception of a saint's life was a detailed description, Jean Goulu reflected consciously and explicitly on the style suited to the kind of book he was writing. If Livy, he says, had had to narrate the life of Jesus or of the apostles, a very different kind of gospel would have resulted. Where men of worldly greatness need biographers of Livy's caliber, a saintly bishop whose conquests and triumphs were confined to the spiritual realm could do with an altogether simpler and less sophisticated *Life*. Like Plutarch in the famous opening passage of his life of Alexander the Great, Jean Goulu could have pointed out that his design was not only to write a *History*, but a *Life*, telling of the soul of the man rather than of the battles he fought; and as the battles for Plutarch, the saint's *gesta* were there for the writer only as a means to an end.

When, however, Goulu disclaims any literary aim at the very beginning in a refreshingly brisk, almost aggressive foreword to the reader, it strikes us as a kind of double bluff, especially in view of the careful structure and the consistent excellence of form of the book.[9] Jean Goulu will forgive us, we hope, if for the purpose of this article we look at his method, and to some extent at his style, so as to make some sort of judgment on his achievement. It is done in the hope of being able to show that even in hagiography literary skill is a desirable asset, and that the lifelike conviction carried by his portrait of Francis de Sales owes much to his expertise as a writer. We do not want to claim it as a hitherto undiscovered masterpiece, but merely to recognize it for what it is: an exceptionally competent and workmanlike book in the true sense of the word. And just because it is really a book, that is, a structural whole, it is in some sense worthy of Francis de Sales himself who was both saint and artist, and who proved in his own works that conscious literary shaping and a pleasing form can add very greatly to the effectiveness of spiritual teaching which draws hearts to the love of God.

Who, then, was Jean Goulu, and what is it that distinguishes his book from the other early *vitae* with which it was associated?

Born in 1576, Jean Goulu[10] was the eldest son of Nicholas Goulu, professor of Greek at the Collège Royal in Paris. His mother, a Greek and Latin scholar in her own right, was the daughter of the humanist, Jean Daurat (or Dorat), who had also held a royal chair in Paris. On his father's death in 1601, Jean, precociously brilliant in his studies, had the chance of following his father in office but he preferred a legal career, embarking on it with every prospect of success and eminence. In the course of the next few years, however, he began to feel the stirrings of a religious vocation and found within himself a strong desire for the ascetic life; so much so that this set up a conflict in his mind with the successful worldly career on which he was now launched. One day when he was pleading a client's cause, his memory suddenly failed him, and being unable to find the thread again, he was forced to give up and leave the court in a state of confusion. Deeply impressed by the precarious nature of human talents and worldly achievement, his mind now turned increasingly and more consciously to spiritual realities. His marked bent for contemplation was fostered by the atmosphere of religious revival and reform in the Paris of his day. This was being brought about by people like Bérulle, Coton, Madame Acarie and her circle, which in 1602 included Francis de Sales, then on a diplomatic mission at the Louvre. Among these people plans were going ahead for the first foundation of St. Teresa's reformed Carmel in France.

One of the most distinguished contemplative congregations in Paris at that time was that of the Feuillants, a reformed branch of the Cistercians, an order dedicated in its primitive austerity to prayer, study, and manual work. The reformer, abbot of the monastery of Notre Dame des Feuillants in the Haute Garonne region, was invited by Henry III to make a foundation in Paris. His entry into the town in 1588 was memorable; the whole court rode out to meet the abbot and his sixty monks who had walked barefoot all the way from the south, not making any change in this austere form of life, eating (on their knees) the sparsest kind of food, drinking water out of skulls and maintaining the strictest silence on the road. The king built a monastery for them close to the royal palaces in the rue Saint Honoré, with land for their farm extending right up to the Tuileries.[11] The congregation prospered and continued to enjoy royal favor; Henry IV laid the foundation stone for the new church in 1601, a splendid library was built up, the monks had a pharmacy, a kind of outpatient clinic for the poor, and by and large the congregation maintained its high standards.

It was the kind of religious order to appeal to a man of Jean Goulu's temperament and intellectual distinction. He entered the Feuillants in 1604 at the age of twenty-eight and was subsequently ordained. His first published work in 1608 was the original French translation from the Greek of the works of Denis the Areopagite, the Neoplatonic mystic so well suited to the cast of Jean Goulu's mind. He did it as a spiritual exercise but also to form his French style. Towards the end of his life he completely revised the translation and it appeared posthumously.[12] It is still most readable and seems hardly to have become dated; he wrote a lucid and harmonious French prose, free of all stylistic affectations, tending, rather, to an austere simplicity. The work was widely known in his time and contributed considerably to the mystical revival, influencing, too, Francis de Sales' own theories in the *Treatise on the Love of God* by drawing his attention to Denis. By 1611, the year in which he first met Francis de Sales in Annecy with a letter of introduction from a close mutual friend in Paris, Jean Goulu was already prior of his monastery. In spite of the burden of administrative work, he continued to publish scholarly books: a translation of Epictetus' *Manual* (1609), commissioned by Marie de Médicis; an edition and translation of Anselm's *Eternal Beatitude*, and also a closely argued work of controversy against a Calvinist minister.[13]

Described as a man of venerable appearance, prematurely white-haired and having an air of great distinction, he won the respect and also the affection of his whole order. In 1622 he was elected Superior General at a chapter meeting of the French and Italian houses of the order at Pinerolo. By command of the Pope, this chapter was presided over by Francis de Sales whose Italian affinities through his sovereign, the Duke of Savoy, made him a suitable choice in this case. Jean Goulu remained in charge for six years, dividing his time between the house of his order in Rome and the French houses, and then retiring to the position of assistant to the new superior. His later years were marked by ill health. Apart from his life of St. Francis de Sales, his one further publication was a polemical and expository work on French style according to the standards laid down by Greek and Latin authors: the *Lettres de Phyllarque*,[14] a sharp attack against Guez de Balzac, published anonymously, though everyone was well able to interpret the pseudonym as *prince des feuilles*. He had hoped to devote his retirement to further literary work, but in a fate which resembles that of Francis de Sales, he was struck down by illness after celebrating Midnight Mass, and died at the age of 53 in the early days of January 1629. All Paris mourned for him, it is related, and there was a great concourse at his funeral.

"This priest, whom I already greatly admired because of the products of his mind I had seen, bound me to love and respect for him with an indissoluble bond when I recognized in him such a great combination of learning, understanding, virtue, piety . . . ,[15] wrote Francis de Sales in 1611 to the friend who had introduced Jean Goulu to him. This high opinion was confirmed over the years, and when, at Pinerolo and then at Turin, Francis de Sales had occasion to live close to him over a period of months in the summer of 1622, he commended him in the highest terms, this time in his official reports to Rome after the election. He described him as being a person "in whom the combination of an exquisite knowledge, of an uncommon prudence, and of an excellent piety existed in beautiful harmony."[16] To a closer friend in Rome, Cardinal Scipio Cobeluzzi, himself a scholar and a patron of the arts, he wrote more freely, in a cry from his own heart, overwhelmed as he had been with administrative work, and yet still cherishing many literary plans.[17] Francis de Sales had gone on writing as long as was humanly possible, though his last completed work, the *Treatise on the Love of God* (1616) dates from six years before his death. He did his best to encourage the new superior to keep on with his writing in spite of other pressures. This is clear from a conversation reported by Jean Goulu, one of the vivid personal touches which abound in his book. One day when Francis had outlined his own extremely comprehensive literary plans—and this talk took place in the summer of 1622, only a few months before his death—the younger man ventured to remark:

> Surely, Monseigneur, this is quite demanding for a man getting on in years and who is not master of all his leisure time. To which he replied with a smile: "True, but to keep your mind in good trim you must always take on much more than you might think yourself capable of actually doing, just as though you still had a long time to live; and yet you mustn't set your heart on achieving any more than if you had to die the very next day.[18]

This was a piece of advice which Jean Goulu often had occasion to remember in the seven busy years yet left to him.

The biography was begun very shortly after Francis' death, the actual commission coming from the bishop's brother and successor, Jean. Louis de Sales supplied material already written up in note form which he had not considered himself capable of turning into a book. The most important source of all has already been mentioned, Madame de Chantal's *mémoires* and her long letter of 1623 to Goulu.[19] From a comparison of what remains of the source material with Jean Goulu's finished book, the most striking thing is that he had completely assimilated the miscellaneous information he was sent, and had sifted and arranged it according to a pattern of his own. He was never content to be merely repetitive; he used direct quotations most judiciously and not merely in order to save himself the trouble of paraphrasing his sources and thus integrating them fully into the scheme of his own text. This is the more striking when compared with Charles-Auguste's method of using a massive barrage of quotations throughout, and also with his naive borrowings—mainly from Goulu—almost always without reference and rarely quite apposite. Jean Goulu's *Life* was distinguished by a strong sense of structure and symmetry, and of what, in his own terms, one might describe as *netteté*.

The work is roughly chronological, arranged in six sections or *livres*, the first three and the last of which tell the saint's life in a time sequence. These sections (1, 2, 3, 6) are of exactly equal length, that is, eighty pages each. Sections 4 and 5 constitute a kind of digression, but so skillful is the narrator and so absorbing his account, that one is scarcely aware of a different tempo. This is the point at which Jean Goulu leaves what one might call the horizontal plane of straight narrative for a dimension of depth. Section 4 is concerned with Francis de Sales' meeting with Madame de Chantal, and with the friendship that resulted in the founding of the Order of the Visitation. This foundation, all that led up to it and all that ensued during the early years of its existence in Annecy, was the most intimate expression of his personality, the thing closest to his heart and therefore the most revealing. Jean Goulu creates an immediately authentic atmosphere, not only by the method of approach, which is discreet, simple and clear, but also by his careful documentation: he gives extracts from personal letters entrusted to him and from some of the characteristic talks, the *Entretiens*, which the saint gave at the Visitation.[20] In this section Goulu gave what was, in fact, the first full account of the origin and nature of an order whose fame was at that time spreading rapidly all over France, and whose foundations totaled some fourteen by the time the book was being written in 1623. The following and fifth section, arising naturally and at the right stage of the book from the description of Francis de Sales' most personal achievement, is devoted to his *estat interieur*, his characteristic spirit and the true nature of his sanctity. Following on Madame de Chantal's analysis in her letter, he finds the secret of this to have consisted in the perfect order and harmony in which the virtues were interrelated and balanced in his personality as a whole.

Expressed in the conventional terms of the genre of the *vita*, the saint's *gesta* are followed by an account of his *virtues*. But how much more subtle is this inner portrait, and how far removed from the usual saint's *vita* where the listed virtues were little more than an *omnium gatherum* of ill assorted material which could not well be fitted in elsewhere. This part of Goulu's book, a true evocation of character systematically developed, fits into the place which is felt to be structurally right for it; it fills in the background which the earlier narrative parts had foreshadowed but not worked out in any detail. While narrative, or *gesta*, can contribute greatly towards the evocation of character, it cannot completely satisfy any but the more unsophisticated demands. In this section the biographer gives himself a chance to cast light on his subject's character from various angles, and the saint is shown in a number of different situations and at several stages of his life, the incidents being chosen to illustrate certain aspects of his personality—humility, patience, forbearance, charity, courage. No anecdote is an end in itself, as it often is in other *vitae*. If, after reading this section, we have the impression of a well-filled and colorful background, we know that the point of it all has nevertheless been to focus more attention on the main figure and throw it up in sharper relief.

Francis de Sales is seen at work in his home at Annecy, receiving a never ending stream of callers (often difficult), and of letters (usually ill written); we follow him out on the road in his mountain diocese, vividly described in Rousseauesque terms on occasion, then we find him preaching in all the large cities of France, at court in Paris or in Turin. He is seen dealing with a great variety of people, the priests and servants of his own household, kings and beggars, innkeepers, penitents, converts, angry detractors and beloved friends, animals, even, whom he handled with Franciscan gentleness. He had a special gift for healing the mentally sick, and Jean Goulu has a number of memorable stories about them. Yet he never allows any of these people, the dangerous madman whom no one dares approach, the unkempt deaf-mute boy, or even the angry abbot, to steal the center of the stage; he sketches them in swiftly so as to show Francis de Sales in a gesture of compassion, patience, or humility. Throughout the section he follows a planned scheme, taking in turn the passions, the cardinal and theological virtues, the charismatic gifts; this is nowhere obtrusive, or indeed, even evident, unless experience of this genre has taught one to look for such a sequence. He uses the same groundwork plan here as Madame de Chantal did in her letter to him; this was his chief source for the inner portrait, but he expanded it considerably from his own observation and with the help of the saint's letters.

This section, and the preceding one on the Visitation, are both longer than the other parts, but again, the balance is carefully considered, and both match one another exactly in length, that is, they are 133 pages each. Structurally, their function is to amplify and complement the narrative parts which precede and follow them. The first three parts tell of the saint's family and birth, his education at Annecy, Paris, and Padua, his vocation to the priesthood (*Livre 1*), his first assignment as a missionary in Calvinist territory near Geneva, and his diplomatic mission to Henry IV (*Livre 2*), his consecration as bishop of Geneva in 1604, his daily life at Annecy, his preaching and writing work, on which Jean Goulu has more pertinent things to say than any of his contemporaries (*Livre 3*). After the intermission of the chronological sequence, and the inner portrait by which the reader has gained the deeper insights described above, he returns (*Livre 6*) to complete the story of the saint's last years, his final stay in Paris for the marriage arranged between the royal houses of France and Savoy, his growing ill health and his last journey to France, again in court service, which ended in his death at Lyons on 28 December 1622. It is told with restraint and simplicity. The account of a personal experience, which Jean Goulu attributes to Francis de Sales' intercession, brings this unusual book to a quiet close.

Lucidity, discretion and a marked power of synthesis are the dominant impressions left in the mind after reading this *Life*. There is no obvious art, nothing contrived, yet there is both elegance and strength in Jean Goulu's presentation of his matter. His characterization of Francis de Sales' preaching and some of the things he says about the *Treatise on the Love of God* show his characteristic way of summarizing impressions.[21] While it is not possible to prove what Francis' *ipsissima verba* were in any given circumstance not witnessed by Goulu himself, one has the impression from comparison with other sources, that he practiced some judicious editing so as to assimilate reported dialogue to his own ideas of neatness and suitability.

He tends to understatement rather than to exaggeration, and on the whole his sentences are brief, though he can, when occasion seems to demand it, launch out into a series of carefully articulated and clearly related clauses. The book is well paragraphed, by no means the rule at that time. Charles-Auguste, for instance, perhaps for reasons of economy, writes his book of six hundred pages without a single paragraph. Goulu rarely allows himself his own personal reflections on what he is narrating, but sees himself purely as an intermediary or a reporter, a feat of detachment of which few preachers of the time—de la Rivière, de Longueterre, and Philibert de Bonneville were all renowned orators—seem to have been capable. But in this book the author's ego does not intrude; all interest centers on the saint and on the nature of his holiness. Goulu had no literary reputation to make by means of this book—he had one; he was devoid of literary vanity and also of the itch to improve a moral occasion, being content to let events speak for themselves and carry their own impact. In this he differs markedly from the writers of the early Baroque who were his contemporaries; he reminds one more of an earlier tradition, of Erasmus, and even of the Tudor *vitae* of Sir Thomas More already mentioned, especially that by Roper. Jean Goulu was too strongly marked by the humanist teaching and discipline of his parents and of the Collège Royal to have permitted himself the stylistic vagaries and excesses of, for instance, de Longueterre. He avoids figurative language, or when he does, on rare occasions, use a metaphor, it is no more than a stock image. He was a lawyer who could write, a sober historian and analyst with an eye for essentials, not ornament. "The perfection of good writing well consists in the fullness (*rondeur*), in the clarity (*netteté*), and in the simplicity of language, with some ornament when the material requires it . . . ,"[22] is how he himself put it. *Pureté* and *netteté* were the essential requisites which Vaugelas considered necessary for good style, the former being concerned with the choice of words and problems of usage, the latter more with arrangement, structure and all that contributes to clarity of expression. *Netteté* does not, however, correspond exactly to clarity, for as Vaugelas points out, a sentence can be clear without being *net*, that is, well constructed. Jean Goulu's scholarly work in other fields shows that he was intensely aware of the importance of *netteté* for good writing. It can be designated as the dominant quality of his style, indeed, of his thought, which is characterized by both *clareté* and *netteté*. It is this quality which makes his book so satisfying and so easy of access to a reader even now.

Goulu considered that language was God's best gift to man and that in its own human way, language stands in the same relation to our reason as the Word does to the Divinity. It is therefore something almost like a religious duty to use words well and for an upright purpose, and the aim of Phyllarque was to help people do just this, to sharpen their critical judgment so that they could learn to distinguish "good" from "bad" both in matter and in form. Phyllarque suggests that when we pick up a new book we should first of all ask ourselves: who is the author, what is he saying, and how does he say it? We then proceed to examine it with regard to "les moeurs, les pensées, l'artifice et les termes."[23] *Les termes* corresponds, as one can see from Phyllarque's development of the idea to Vaugelas' *pureté* and the whole field of good usage. In the same way, the concept of *artifice* leads him on to *netteté*, that is, to structure in the widest sense.

Claude Favre de Vaugelas belonged to the same circle in Paris as the Feuillant General. He was the son of President Antoine Favre, Francis de Sales' most intimate friend in Annecy; and his sister, Mère Marie Jacqueline Favre, was one of the first Visitation nuns and superior of the Paris monastery later on. It has not been possible to discover any record of a meeting or of correspondence between Vaugelas and Jean Goulu, nor does this matter; it is evident they shared the same linguistic preoccupations. There was the same aversion to affectation and vain display, the same desire, expressed in similar terms, for *pureté* and *netteté*. Some years before the publication of Vaugelas' treatise in 1647, Phyllarque's critical letters, subtitled *où il est traité de l'eloquence françoise*, enjoyed a tremendous vogue; they were compulsory reading matter in every salon, produced in fine bindings for this purpose, and even sent off from Paris in cartloads so as to supply bright young officers with suitable reading when they were out on maneuvers or actually engaged in war. True, the scandal of Phyllarque's bold attack on a writer as popular as Balzac had something to do with making these letters a best-seller; but their virulence has been much exaggerated, while their serious quality as a treatise on style has been underestimated. A careful analysis of the letters from this point of view would be a worthwhile task. Jean Goulu's greatest literary effort, his *Vie du bien-heureus Messire François de Sales*, would then be seen as a work which puts his own teaching into practice, and does it well.

NOTES

1. Dom Jean de Saint François, *La vie du bien-heureus Messire François de Sales* (Paris, 1624; second edition 1625; reprinted 1725), 589 pp. (hereafter *Vie)* It was reprinted twice thereafter as the introduction to a collected edition of the saint's works: *Oeuvres complètes de Saint François de Sales*, 6 vols. (Bar-le-Duc, 1868, and also Paris, 1884). I have not been able to find a copy of Goulu's work in England. The Bibliothèque Nationale has the 1625 edition only, inscribed: "Bibliotheca Fulientina Coenobii S. Bernadini Pariensis." The 1624 edition was made available to me by the kindness of the Paris Visitation.

2. Sieur de Longueterre, *La vie du tres-illustre Messire François de Sales* (Lyons, 1624), 972 pp. Part II is entitled "Les Souspirs de Philothée." The Cambridge University Library has a complete copy, but the Bibliothèque Nationale only has the dedicatory epistle of the funeral oration entitled *Harangue funebre prononcée sur la mort de nostre Rssme Pere en Dieu Messire François de Sales Evesque et Prince de Geneve* (Lyons, 1623), not the oration itself.

3. Louis de la Rivière, *La vie de l'Illustrissime et Reverendissime François de Sales* (Lyons, 1624). Further editions in 1625, 1626, 1627, and 1631. The British Museum has the 1627 edition.

4. Philibert de Bonneville, *Abregé de la vie du bienheurueus François de Sales* (Lyons, 1623), 128 pp. *La vie du bienheureux François de Sales* (Lyons, 1628), 537 pp.

5. "Déposition de Sainte Chantal pour la canonisation de Saint François de Sales." First published in Louis Joseph de Baudry, *Divers suppléments aux oeuvres de Saint François de Sales* (Lyons, 1836). Reprinted in Migne, *Oeuvres complètes de Ste Jeanne Françoise de Chantal*, vol. 1 (Paris, 1862). The further

editions of the "Déposition" (Annecy, 1876 and 1923, and Namur, 1960) are not critical editions like that of de Baudry. The present writer's translation of the text of the *Testimony*, checked by MS sources, was published in 1967, the fourth centenary year of St. Francis de Sales' birth (London: Faber and Faber/Hyattsville: Institute of Salesian Studies).

6. Charles-Auguste de Sales, *De Vita et rebus gestis. . . Francisci Salesii* (Lyons, 1634), 490 pp. *Histoire du bien-heureux François de Sales*, composée premierement en latin par son nepveu Charles-August de Sales et mise in françois par le mesme auteur (Lyons, 1634). Reprinted Paris, 1866, 2 vols.

7. Jean-Pierre Camus, *L'Esprit du bien-heureux François de Sales*, 6 vols. (Paris, 1640). Reprinted Paris, 1840, 3 vols., 1546 pp. The frequently reprinted selection by P. M. Collott ("P.M.C."), first published in Paris, 1725, is unrepresentative and does not do justice to this remarkable work.

8. Erasmus, *Virorum qui superiori nostroque seculo eruditione . . . et doctrina illustres atque memorabiles fuerunt Vitae* (Frankfurt, 1536). The brief life of Thomas More by his son-in-law, William Roper, and the fuller life by Nicholas Harpsfield, both written ca. 1556-67, have appeared in the E.E.T.S. Series, in 1935 and 1932 respectively, and have been published in a modern translation in Everyman's Library: William Roper and Nicholas Harpsfield, *Lives of Saint Thomas More*, edited with an introduction by E. E. Reynolds (1963).

9. *Vie*, Au Lecteur.

10. The sources for Jean Goulu's life are not plentiful. There is some information in the Latin elogium appended to the second and posthumous edition of his translation of Denys the Areopagite (see note 12 below), also in Bayle's *Dictionnaire historique et critique (1730)*, in the *Nouvelle Biographie Générale* and the *Biographie Universelle*. The information in these general

reference books is colored by the tendentious account of him by his enemy, La Motte-Aigron, who took the part of Guez de Balzac in the literary battle between Goulu and Balzac. A nephew, Nicholas Goulu, is said to have written an account of his uncle in a Latin elogium of various members of his family (1653), but I have not been able to find any trace of this. For a recent account of the Feuillant order, see the article by Maur Standaert in the *Dictionnaire de Spiritualité*, vol. 5 (Paris, 1964), 274-87.

11. The Feuillant monastery with its extensive grounds was situated on the present site of the rue Castiglione and a part of the rue de Rivoli adjoining the Tuileries gardens and still called "Terrasse des Feuillants." Anne d'Autriche had a covered passageway constructed from the palace to the Feuillant church. This church was destroyed after the Revolution in the course of which it served as a meeting place for a group of politicians known as "le club Feuillant."

12. *Oeuvres de Saint Denys Areopagite.* Seconde traduction (Paris, 1642).

13. *Reponse au livre de la Vocation des Pasteurs de Pierre du Molin, Ministre de Charenton* (Paris, 1620).

14. *Lettres de Phyllarque a Ariste*, où il est traitié de l'eloquence françoise, 2 vols. (Paris, 1627-28, and subsequent editions).

15. *Oeuvres*, 25:78.

16. *Oeuvres*, 20:321.

17. *Oeuvres*, 20:323.

18. *Vie*, 233.

19. *Ste. Jeanne Françoise Frémyot de Chantal: Sa vie et ses oeuvres*, 8 vols. (Paris, 1874-90), 3:245 ff. For centuries this letter has

formed the traditional preface to selections of St. Francis de Sales' letters. See the present writer's "A Character Sketch of St. Francis de Sales: St. Chantal's Letter of December, 1623, to Dom Jean de Saint-François," *Salesian Studies*, vol. 3, no. 1 (Winter 1966): 44-55, and translation of St. Chantal's *Testimony* (see note 5 above), 165-72.

20. These talks were unpublished at the time when Jean Goulu's biography appeared and were therefore a novel and attractive feature of the book. They were edited as *Les Vrays Entretiens spirituels* (Lyons, 1629).

21. *Vie*, 150-51, 524-25, respectively.

22. *Lettres de Phyllarque*, 1:10.

23. *Lettres de Phyllarque*, 2:51.

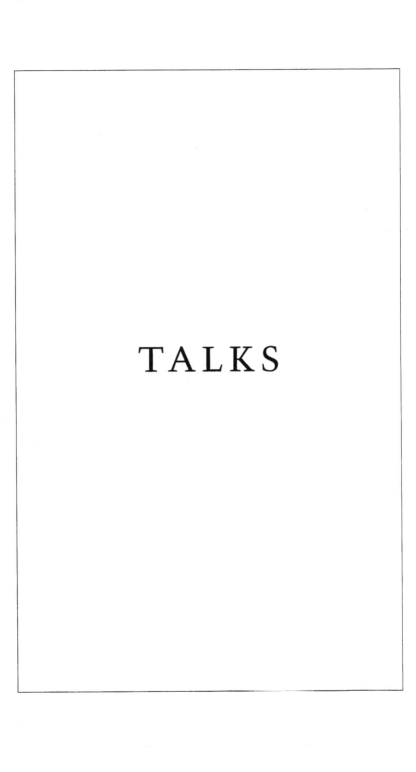

TALKS

VII

MEDIEVAL AFFINITIES: ST. FRANCIS OF ASSISI

François de Sales' pattern of holiness belonged, essentially, to the time and the spirit of the Counter Reformation and the aftermath of the Council of Trent (1545-1563). Charles Borromeo, the Italian saint on whom François modeled himself in his pastoral and diocesan role, was still alive when François was born in Savoy, and was canonized in the year when François and Madame de Chantal founded the Visitation Order in 1610. Philip Neri (1515-1595), whose Oratory and whole spiritual approach were of great significance for François was canonized, as also was Teresa of Ávila, in 1622, the year of his death. Then there were the great Jesuit saints of an earlier generation, perhaps closest of all to François de Sales by virtue of his education and a lifelong allegiance: Ignatius of Loyola himself, Francis Xavier, Peter Canisius with whom François actually corresponded, as he did with Robert Bellarmine, the outstanding theologian and polemicist of his time.

These names have been listed so as to place François in his right setting among people with whom he has much in common though he was the only Frenchman among them. Even so, as a Savoyard, he also had strong Italian affinities, not only through his studies in Padua but by his allegiance to an Italian court in Turin, the far side of the Alps: his Italian was as fluent as his French, and Italy and the Italian landscape were to him a home from home. In spite of all his resemblance to these Counter-Reformation saints—his effective missionary work, his pastoral reforms of episcopal and clerical practice, his immensely successful renewal of lay spirituality—the impression grows as one gets to know him better in his books and in his letters that there were also marked differences and that there is somehow a different feel and atmosphere about his sanctity which goes beyond a mere difference of temperament and personality. It is doubtful whether, even in his own time, he was seen as really modern and contemporary, in spite of all his meticulous putting into practice of all that was new and rightly "modern" in the post-Tridentine epoch to which he belonged. He has, I think, a marked affinity with some of the medieval and late medieval saints, some of the holy men and women to whose example and sayings he refers so constantly in his books and in his letters of direction. It is natural, even inevitable, that he should point to established earlier patterns of holiness; all the same, he seems so very close to them in spirit, always eager for his readers to share his own delight in them as models so clearly in harmony with his own attitudes. He read and reread the story of their lives, an early *vita* was the usual appointed reading aloud at the bishop's table at Annecy, he was always recommending such books in his letters and he told countless anecdotes from them to illustrate points in his books and in his sermons.

I'm thinking of saints like St. Martin of Tours, for instance, from whom he quoted even on his deathbed, St. Bernard of Clairvaux from Madame de Chantal's own region of Burgundy, or St. Anselm of Canterbury—Francis liked to remind people that "this most sympathetic saint" was a native of Aosta in Savoy. There were the two Catherines, of Siena and of Genoa, St. Elisabeth of Hungary, the exemplary wife, mother and widow, St. Louis, King of France, and his wife, Margaret of Provence, unforgettably described in a parable of total trust of God's guiding Providence during their journey to the Holy Land at the time of the Crusades (*Treatise*, Bk. 9, ch. 13). But most important of all to François de Sales, there was the poor man of Assisi, "mon cher patron," as he always called him. The chronicle of St. Francis' life by another favorite saint, St. Bonaventure, the *Fioretti* or "Little Flowers" (1322), that is, the legends about St. Francis and his early companions, were written in his heart from childhood, quite simply a part of his life and of his thinking, always at the tip of his tongue or of his pen; his special

love went out to St. Francis' own writings, the *Lauds*, with "The
Canticle of Brother Sun" (1225).[1] Both François de Sales' parents
were named after this saint, as was the room where their son was
born. The castle of Thorens has long vanished except for this one
room which has been turned into a chapel dedicated both to
François and to his "cher patron." This chapel on the hillside of a
mountain valley is overshadowed by great lime trees said to be
centuries old and now the haunt of bees: hives have been put
near the chapel, in celebration of the symbolism of the bee greatly
loved by both saints.

Four hundred years separated François de Sales from his
patron saint (1181-1226) just as there are now nearly four
centuries between us and François. One is rather apt to telescope
past centuries and thus not to see the time factor in quite
right perspective; but correctly situating such points of time is
important, if only as an aid towards really understanding just how
radical was the change of consciousness brought about by the
Counter Reformation in the religious attitudes and thinking of
Europe. It was the great divide between late medieval times and
what we can already see as something like a "modern" era. Other
religious writers of François' own century and epoch did not
bridge this transition point in the same smooth and gradualist
way: without being traditionalist in a negative way, he was not
"modern" either in his own time. There was, perhaps, something
rather timeless, and this was, I think, because he was a man of
the soil, of the land, a mountain tree as he liked to call himself,
no sophisticated townee, not at home in a great capital city like
Paris or Turin: "je suis des champs," he used to say, "I'm a country
cousin." Perhaps this is what makes him move so easily and
happily among saints of a much earlier epoch than his own and
to cultivate their memory by a marked preference.

A factor which strengthens this impression is his constant use
of comparisons from fabled animal and nature lore, from medieval
bestiaries, to illustrate moral and psychological situations that he
was trying to explain.[2] This is less naive than it may look; it was
an element of literary conservationism which has not often been
recognized as such. The man who could revel in the use of these
images was also the writer who, in the first four books of the
Treatise on the Love of God, could subject his readers to some very

abstruse philosophical, scholastic argument and reasoning. But to the medieval eye of faith,—and François was consciously exploring and exploiting this—every possible and impossible animal in the world as described by bestiaries concealed some hidden message and meaning to be deciphered in the Book of Nature. St. Augustine, that sophisticated intellectual, commenting on the great textbook of animal lore, the *Physiologus*, said that it mattered not at all whether certain of these animals existed: the important thing is what they meant, and what, through them, could be vividly imagined. All this coincided with François' own taste and with his consistent technique as a writer and preacher intent on making the life of the spirit comprehensible and attractive to his readers and listeners: it was no spurious romanticism.

The marvelous freshness and joy of François' completely unsentimental attitude, not only to nature itself but to the fictions about the nature of an epoch much earlier than his own, continually remind us of his patron saint's love of all God's creation: in this he is truly "Franciscan." He tells of St. Francis' Canticle of the Sun in the *Laude* and about what he calls his "hundred other benedictions on creatures, all of whom he calls brothers and sisters, asking them to come to the help of his own poor heart, languishing because he was not able to praise his soul's beloved Savior as fully and as well as he longed to do" (*Treatise*, Bk. 5, ch. 9). François sees his patron as a "sacred nightingale," the more its delight in its song of praise, the greater its grief in the limits of its power. Adrien Gambart, in his emblem-book *Vita* of François de Sales (1664), thinks that François has drawn his own portrait there, that he is, in fact, another Francis of Assisi, "expressing himself perfectly in the symbol of these little songsters of heaven, caroling out their praise of God night and day without ceasing" (see Plate 7).[3] "Worthy indeed are these birds of the fair name of Philo-mel, lovers of song and melody, for they even die for the love of their song of praise," François writes in the *Treatise* (Bk. 5, ch. 8). Gambart does not hesitate to make this identification of the two saints and work it out in detail, across the gap of four centuries and more. On François' part, too, seeing his saint in the image of a singing bird consumed by the fervor and beauty of its own melody, had about it a touch of nostalgia for medieval times lost forever, a harking back to what looked like a golden age of simple faith so perfectly embodied and expressed in the saint of Assisi. It is with such thoughts in mind that today's reader can most fruitfully approach and understand François de Sales' own conscious and deliberately used imagery in his writings and his sermons.

In the *Treatise* (Bk. 7, ch. 11) François tells of his patron's seraphic love of God which marked him with the signs, or "stigmata" of Christ's Passion, marking and branding him with a shared and piercing pain, a union with Our Lord's suffering. Then he tells of St. Francis' humility, again explaining the literal meaning of that word, from the Latin *humus*, the ground, the earth, when he asked to be laid on bare earth when he came to die: "the great St. Francis who is always in my mind's eye when there is talk of heavenly love, this man who honestly thought himself the chief of all sinners, a fact which I see as an oracle of this great doctor of the science of saints, a man whose love was nurtured and nourished in the school of the crucifix." And his love of the Child Jesus in the stall at Bethlehem also called him to a total humility, to abjection and to complete unworldliness. François sees that his patron's love of true humility, of suffering, went hand in hand with joy and peace so that the marks of Our Lord's Passion were accepted and welcomed with happiness as the sign of the closest possible identification with his master. This is what made the deepest impression on François de Sales and what is also most evident in his own life and its closeness to a truly Franciscan poverty insofar as he was able to combine his lifestyle with what was owing to his position as Prince Bishop of Geneva. He welcomed suffering of every kind, even penury, yet all this was closely hidden and unspectacular, hardly even known or suspected by those very close to him: the expression on his face was always one of calm acceptance, of serenity, he radiated peace. His patron was his lifelong model of joyful identification with his suffering Lord.

The witnesses at François' canonization process, especially the members of his own household who were in the best position to observe hidden maneuvers, are unanimous in their testimony about his quite extraordinary love of "Lady Poverty": the small room where he worked and also slept (minimally), his plain fare, his lavish almsgiving, whether or not he had what his bursar considered the wherewithal, and whether or not all the beggars deserved his generosity; he endlessly gave them the benefit of the doubt, the only solution, as he pointed out, if love is your all, as it was for his patron and his model. He rejoiced when he himself was badly treated, not given due honor, kept waiting as a poor outsider, even, outside his own lodging: he refused actually to own a house, he was a lifelong lodger, he courteously refused lavish gifts and large stipends—it was all as "Franciscan" as any bishop of that epoch could possibly have made it, and get away with it. He is perhaps at his most Franciscan when he is walking in all weathers, staff in hand, along the more remote mountain paths of his diocese, visiting the poorest and the most lonely members of his flock, sharing sorrows and anxieties as one of them, speaking their dialect, bringing comfort and hope. It is not possible to read such accounts of Alpine visits and not be thinking, too, of the wild solitude of Alverna in the Appenines, and the hardship and suffering it meant. But peace and serenity in suffering remained unruffled right to the end, when he stood bareheaded on the steps of Lyons cathedral in an icy December wind, taking part in court ceremonial and in conversation with royalty and church dignitaries. He died shortly afterwards in the gardener's cottage on the grounds of the Lyons Visitation monastery, having declined, on the occasion of this important visit to the city to make use of the fine lodging assigned to him: he died in a setting of poverty and solitude.

Remembering Alverna, one could go on to say that St. Francis was also, perhaps, a model of contemplative prayer to François (and through him, to the Visitation order), not perhaps the very first thing one might now call to mind in connection with the poor man of Assisi. But in the *Treatise* and often elsewhere, he tells of the long nights St. Francis spent in prayer, repeating over and over again, till dawn came, "O God, You are my God and my all!" And as his patron had hidden himself away, at the end, at Alverna, "a holy place most proper for contemplation, solitary and remote," so François longed in his last years to retire to Talloires, the hermitage of St. Germain in the rock caves overlooking the Lake of Annecy and the mountains, there to pray and write, to go on using his beads and his pen as long as he could, giving all he now had left to give as he hurried from the world of time to the timeless realm of eternity. His attribute in pictures and statues was, and still now is, his quill pen to symbolize his apostolate of writing, while the beads point to his unceasing prayer which is what inspired and gave meaning to his writing and authorship. His prayer became increasingly, throughout his life, the mystical prayer of simplicity in which, as we are told of his patron in the *Vita*, "he was already made a fellow-citizen with the angels in the heavenly mansions, ever seeking his Beloved from whom the wall of flesh alone parted him."[4] "Contemplative," or mystical prayer in the manner of the saint of Assisi was not ever, and certainly not before the Counter Reformation, seen as exclusive territory for cloistered élite: it was for all who loved God in real earnest, whether religious or lay people.

François de Sales is generally marked out as having been among the first to stress the need for true devotion among lay people and even to demand their perfection. There is perhaps some truth in that for his own late sixteenth-century epoch: even there it tends to be forgotten that St. Ignatius composed his *Spiritual Exercises* as an instrument of conversion for lay people, a program which François worked out in greater detail and with much additional matter as a great spiritual keep-fit course, a course "given" by a personal director to the lay person wanting to love God more, to live the good life. However, four centuries before the *Introduction to the Devout Life*, St. Francis and his uncloistered friars converted such a great crowd of quite ordinary everyday Christians by their preaching and example that these people had to be organized into a lay order, the Order of Penance, the first of the Third Orders, together, too, with the similar Tertiaries, as they were then called, of the Dominican Order. These people, looking for a greater spiritual challenge, are now called "Lay Franciscans" and "Lay Dominicans," while in François' time the "Philotheas" and "Théotimes" were simply seen as "devout," as following a way of "true devotion," to which a book, addressed to them personally, has "introduced" them. Over and over again he gives these people who are trying to live a life of greater commitment the great example of his own patron, ending his book with a quotation taken from the *Fioretti*, rendered in the first English recusant translation of the *Introduction* (London, 1616) by the attractive jingle-couplet: "Since heaven is for my pains assigned, Pains are sweet past-time to my mind," for François' "Et quand la peine de la vie dévote vous semblera dure, chantez avec saint François: "A cause des biens que j'attends, Les travaux me sont passe-tempe"—lines taken from the First Consideration of the Stigmata, in the *Fioretti*.[5] There are constant echoes, too, of the narrative, legend-style approach of the *Fioretti* in François' book and in its whole atmosphere. Where other spiritual writers of his time tend to keep to straight exposition in developing an argument, a teaching, François varies his approach: he rings the changes with anecdotes, imaginary dialogues, conversational asides, and above all, with vivid parables of his own invention. He readily takes quite long stories, for instance, from St. Bernardine of Siena, a Franciscan preacher, who tells of a pilgrim to the Holy Land who died of the love of God when he reached the Garden of Olives (*Treatise*, Bk. 7, ch. 12); and he comes back again and again to the most beloved lay Franciscan of her time, St. Elisabeth of Hungary.

Reminiscent, too, of François' love of his patron, was his attitude to animals, not only in their more lyrical aspects, as in St. Francis preaching to his birds, or St. Anthony of Padua and his attentive audience of fish on the seashore, but to animals or the animal spirit in its fierceness and savagery. François was known to have great power over people who were possessed or unbalanced in a wild and dangerous way, just as his patron had the power to deal with the wolf of Gubbio—very probably just a very sick man, a mental case, terrorizing the neighbourhood, but represented, in that famous statue in Assisi, as the wolf, tamed by the fearless love and pity of a saint. So much that one reads of in what might be called the *Fioretti* of St. François de Sales, an account of his miracles and healings as told by contemporaries,[6] is more closely kindred to medieval lore than to the more stern and sophisticated atmosphere of the "Grand Siècle" in France, as also to the more unconcessive and intransigent Counter-Reformation mentality. A clearer realization of this medieval "Franciscan" affinity could also lead to a less sentimental understanding of François' famous quality of *douceur*, much misunderstood and untranslatable, though "gentleness" will have to do as a poor attempt, hiding as it does, the strength within the sweetness. A sentimentalized image is as wrong for François de Sales as it is for St. Francis of Assisi.

NOTES

1. See St. Francis of Assisi and others, *The Little Flowers, Legends and Lauds*, edited by Otto Karrer and translated by N. Wydenbruck (1947; London, 1984).

2. See the well illustrated *The Bestiary: A Book of Beasts*, being a translation from a Latin Bestiary of the Twelfth Century, made and edited by T. H. White (1954; New York: Capricorn Books, 1960). The original MS is in the Cambridge University Library.

3. *La Vie Symbolique du bienheureux François de Sales, comprise sous le voile de 52 Emblèmes* (Paris, 1664), emblem 48.

4. *The Little Flowers*, 257.

5. Ibid., 244.

6. *Pouvoir de Saint François de Sales*. Miracles et Guérisons opérées par le Saint Evêque (Bourg, 1865; newly edited 1911).

VIII

SPANISH LINKS: ST. FRANCIS DE SALES AND ST. TERESA OF ÁVILA

Throughout his life St. Francis de Sales had close links with the spirituality of St. Ignatius of Loyola: at the Jesuit college of Clermont during his school-days in Paris, at the university of Padua where he lived under the direction of the Jesuit writer and missionary, Antonio Possevino, and, finally, year by year through the *Spiritual Exercises* which he made under Jesuit direction throughout his career as Bishop of Geneva. In view of these close ties, one might well expect a talk about "Spanish Links" to begin with a closer look at St. Francis' attitude towards St. Ignatius. But in his case the link was less directly with the saint himself; it was with the Society of Jesus as a whole and at a time when the Jesuits were already an established European and worldwide phenomenon. At that point their particular and characteristic spirituality no longer came across as something specifically "Spanish." But St. Francis' contacts with St. Teresa herself and with her reformed Carmel in France not long after the saint's death in 1582 were a quite different case. Here the connections were immediate through St. Teresa's writings, and were important in specific, tangible ways.[1]

There are two ways of approaching a topic of this kind: by a detailed comparison of the writings of both saints, or by comparing their general approach, their personality and achievement within the historical setting in their own very different countries, or, more specifically, in the context of the Counter Reformation as a whole. In a short talk the comparison can only be *grosso modo*—a favorite term of St. Francis when he was short of time—that is, as between two people dealing with specific problems, each in their own sphere, but—and this is important—who were both outstanding writers, artists of genius, so that we can approach them in an immediate way even now, four centuries later. St. Teresa reformed her own order—and under obedience wrote an account of what she did—renewing the contemplative mystical life of prayer, while St. Francis de Sales tackled the situation by working resolutely at the reform of religious houses in his diocese, but also by founding his own "institute," as he called it, the Visitation Order. In his two great books, he first of all "introduced" people to the devout life and then followed on with a "treatise" on the love of God, showing souls the way to a deeper life of prayer in a totally committed, though not necessarily cloistered life.

Anyone who knows St. Francis de Sales well and discovers St. Teresa at a later stage, as was my own case, feels immediately at home and in a familiar atmosphere; this applies in spite of all the very real differences, herself a cloistered nun in the heart of Spain, he a highly placed ecclesiastic responsible for a diocese strongly infiltrated by militant Calvinism. Whereas she was concerned only with the formation and spirituality of her own order, his main responsibility was for the parishes, priests and people of Savoy, and only in the second place for the reformation of monasteries and for training the order he founded together with Madame de Chantal. He was an academic, a conscious, often sophisticated writer in the humanist and baroque mode, trained in the art of rhetoric and of oratory from the time of his Jesuit schooling. St. Teresa was what she called "unlettered," that is, a more or less untutored natural writer, but a born writer all the same, whose work, it must be stressed, though written under obedience and at odd moments of an intensely busy, hardworking career as a foundress, did have the benefit of scholarly revision and editing by a learned adviser, the Augustinian friar Luis de León. Her teaching was based on her own personal experience because this is what she was told to write about; St. Francis' writings, though all the time of course revealing his own heart and soul, were in the first place for "Philothea" and for "Théotime," the soul that loves God, the soul that has learnt the fear of God. But in neither of these two writers are there any watertight compartments, no hedging off of the mystical from the ascetic sphere: both of them have far too much plain common sense, one might say, for that kind of rigid classification. The concept of "devotion" in St. Francis' first publication of 1608 is inseparable from the "love of God" in the title of his second work of 1616; both works were synchronized and in fact coincided in the time of their writing.

The bridging factor here was the Visitation, founded at a midpoint of time between the two main books. It could be said that he was all the time passing the contemplative spirituality of the cloister on to the devout living a lay life in the world and for whom there was so little specific, practical instruction. Of course St. Teresa too, knew all about such people, had them constantly in mind and in her parlor; that was why she had a shrewd and compassionate insight into their difficulties, their plight: "I'm really sorry for spiritual people who for certain pious reasons are obliged to go on living in the world," she says (*Life*, ch. 37): "the cross they have to bear is a dreadful one." She is thinking of those who, in St. Francis' words, "live in cities, in their families, hedged round by household cares, people at court or in the press of public affairs. . . It is a mistake, indeed a heresy, to want to banish the devout life—from the army, the workshop, the homes of married people" (*Introduction*, Part 1, ch. 3). Even from brief quotations like this it is clear how vividly both these saints come across as people in what they are saying. In their own age and ever after, both have enjoyed immense popularity as real living people, as friends, in their writings; every reader has the impression we know them personally, as indeed we do. "Notre chère Mère Thérèse," as Francis called her, was a real and beloved friend to him, to his correspondents and to every Visitandine when he wrote and spoke about her. What is the historical setting of this warm affinity between two people who later on were both named Doctors of the Church, true "doctors" in the original connotation of the word, who teach so much, and so well about the love of God, of His creation, His creatures?

How and when did Francis de Sales come to know Teresa of Ávila? The early years of his priestly career were filled with missionary zeal for the return of heretics to the one true Church, and this was after more than a century had passed in embattled attitudes of hostility since the beginning of the Reformation. Francis had learnt much not only *about* Luther and Calvin but *from* them and from the life of the people in his diocese, a large Protestant presence always there before him and in control of his own see, his cathedral in Geneva. This Calvinist presence showed him a religious world with few clergy, no monks, friars or nuns, and where responsibility for things religious was virtually in the hands of committed lay people, not of ministers. He saw how many were attracted to Calvinism by their longing for a deeper religious life, for an inner piety of a kind perhaps more rarely found outside the cloister in Catholic lands. At the same time the great majority of religious houses, whether male or female, were in a state of sad disarray, crying out for reformation. Francis de Sales therefore had two basic desires and aims: he wanted to help and to instruct lay people, to show them that "perfection" was not a prerogative of the cloister or of the priestly state, that it could and should go together with a wholehearted and deepened understanding of the moral duties of one's state of life, a life to be led in ever greater dependence on God in loving prayer and self-sacrifice. And then, by his writing, teaching and practical administrative skill (he was a trained lawyer as well as a theologian), he wanted to work towards the reform of religious houses already in existence, and to introduce new and reformed orders from abroad. In the case of his own Savoy, this meant more especially an influx from Italy in the shape of the Capuchins, and the teaching orders—the Ursulines and Theatines, while for France, in the religious welfare of which he was, of course, also greatly concerned, these same orders were involved, but closest of all to his heart was the reformed Carmel of St. Teresa, the mystical invasion from Spain.

After five years of missionary work in the Chablais Francis was appointed coadjutor to the aging Bishop of Geneva; in 1602 he was sent on a diplomatic mission to the court of Henry of Navarre, Henry IV, in Paris. Returning home at the end of that year with many new ideas and new friends, he was himself consecrated bishop of Geneva following the death of Bishop Granier. In the home of Madame Barbe Acarie, a spiritual salon, as one might call it, he met a group of people who were instrumental in founding Carmels in France and who had contacts in Spain with people who had actually known St. Teresa, St. John of the Cross, and, more especially, Mother Anne of Jesus (de Lobera), the most beloved and trusted of Mother Teresa's spiritual daughters. This meant that for the first time Francis found himself in living and immediate contact with Teresa of Ávila and all she stood for. Among those he met in Madame Acarie's house, and perhaps most important of all to him, was Jean de Brétigny, half-French, half-Spanish, whose translations—excellent and reliable, and this is of the greatest importance—of Teresa's *Life* (written from 1562-65) and *Way of Perfection* (1566?) had appeared in 1601, the year before Francis de Sales' sojourn in Paris; the *Foundations* (written from 1573-82) by another translator followed later, in 1616. I am assuming that you, as Carmelites, know all about Acarie, who herself became a Carmelite and died in the odor of sanctity at the Carmel she and her own daughters founded. There was also Brétigny's niece, Charlotte, invaluable because she too was a Spanish speaker, who herself entered Carmel and accompanied Mother Anne of Jesus on her foundation travels in France. Houses were founded in Paris and at Pontoise, and, most important of all as far as Francis de Sales was concerned, at Dijon in Burgundy, in 1605. Like the Visitation, Carmel had a great vogue in seventeenth-century France, also among English Recusants in France and Belgium; by the end of the century Carmel and the Visitation had over a hundred houses in France alone. The spread of both, in Italy, Poland, and of course Spain, where the Visitation was, and still is, in high regard, was phenomenal; Spanish South America, too, has many Visitation monasteries.

For Francis de Sales, his first reading of Mother Teresa and at the same time meeting with a living tradition of the saint herself and of her reform, meant a great enrichment of his own spirituality which in spite of all his extroverted commitments and administrative work, had been steadily developing in a mystical direction. And whereas during his missionary years he had been mainly concerned with exposition of doctrine and dogma in flysheets delivered from house to house, and also in a treatise on the controversial subject of images, *Defense of the Standard of the Holy Cross* (1600), by the time he got to Paris he was free for a different kind of apostolate. He could devote himself to the direction of lay people. In the Acarie circle and at court he was in immediate and great demand as a spiritual director; these years, too, saw the beginning of his great spiritual correspondence to which he devoted himself quite literally to his dying day. At the same time he read not only the works of St. Teresa herself insofar as they were available to him in translation but he also read Ribera's *Vita* of her which had appeared in French in that same year, 1601. It is easy to imagine just how heartening this great personal and spiritual encounter turned out to be for a young gifted cleric of thirty-five, now faced with a whole set of new and intensively demanding spiritual responsibilities. This was the time when he first heard the authentic voice, as one might say, of "Our blessed Mother Teresa," as her friends in Paris called her. He did not, at that point, as yet read Spanish fluently, though later on, when Spanish soldiers were for years stationed at Annecy and also in Turin, Francis de Sales' court of the Duke of Savoy, he made friends and disciples among the Spaniards and acquired a good speaking knowledge of the language. And this makes all the difference for entering into the real spirit and texture of what a writer is saying, even if you have to read him or her in translation. I'm saying this because I want you to try and read Francis de Sales, in his own language, even if you have no more than school French, because he has not been as well served in his translators over the centuries as have the Spanish mystics. But that's by the way.

In 1604 Bishop Francis de Sales was invited to preach a course of Lenten sermons at Dijon cathedral. One of several reasons why he accepted this invitation was the fact that a Carmelite foundation had been proposed for the capital of Burgundy, a Carmel which came into being on 21 September the following year, 1605. The foundress was Mother Anne of Jesus herself, assisted by Charlotte de Brétigny, who was by then Sister Marie de la Trinité. The widowed daughter of President Frémyot, a civic post corresponding to that of the Lord Mayor, was Madame de Chantal, then in her early thirties. She and her young children—her husband had been killed in a hunting accident three years previously—were then living in the castle of Monthelon near Dijon with a difficult old father-in-law. She was pious, devoted to good works and deeply interested in prayer. The story of the meeting between her and Francis de Sales and of how he took on her direction after the Lenten retreat in Dijon is too well known to need retelling here: all the letters, or most of them, which he wrote to her from 1604 until the Visitation was founded in Annecy on Trinity Sunday, 1610, are there for anyone to follow the story of this gradually unfolding contemplative vocation. After his death in 1622 all her letters—he had kept them—were returned to her and she saw fit to burn them. One gets rather weary of the emotional regret lavished on this, as I see it, most understandable and justifiable action on her part. His letters are in any case such that it is not difficult to reconstruct all one needs to know about this missing dimension but without any indiscreet violation of her privacy and her crises of conscience. She wanted to be and to remain hidden, and in spite of her fame and renown all over France in later years—she was called and looked on as the "Mother Teresa" of her own country—she succeeded in remaining essentially hidden which is all to the good.

Madame de Chantal—this is how, as a lady of baronial rank she continued to be known even after she entered religion—and her friends in Dijon, among whom were several other correspondents of Francis de Sales, were ardent supporters and visitors of the new Carmel. Teresa's *Life* and *Way of Perfection* were in all hands and so was her *Interior Castle* when and as the director permitted it to be read. Discretion was very much indicated; wisely and tenderly, Francis helped Madame de Chantal to exercise realistic restraint in her devotional life and practice, and in this St. Teresa herself was of course the best guide and teacher. Reference to her writings are frequent in his letters, perhaps the most significant was the suggestion that Madame de Chantal should read and reread chapters 29 and 30 of the *Way of Perfection*, with the idea of helping her to understand what the presence of God in the soul really meant in common-sense terms. She was to be rescued from her anxious and often compulsive worrying about her prayer and her life in general: "Am I doing the thing properly? Am I really getting it right?" He wanted her to see that all this questioning was a sheer waste of time and spiritual energy. "Let go and let God" was the great lesson he wanted her to understand with the help of Mother Teresa. She was to enter into the happy freedom of God's children, a far more relaxed state of confidence and trust, the *grosso modo*, as he called it, for the life of prayer and total commitment. Who better than St. Teresa to second and explain in her own forthright, commonsense terms such teaching? Though Jeanne de Chantal had other and really frightening problems, her lifelong doubts against the faith, for instance, her ever increasing aridity and desolation, the chief focus of her anxiety in these earlier years was the nature of her prayer. This is where Francis de Sales had firm advice and counsel often coinciding almost word for word with St. Teresa's own findings, refreshingly forthright and informal for those days of an over intellectualized approach to prayer: "I think mental prayer is just treating God as our friend, talking often and alone with Him who loves us, as we know so well . . . the great thing is not to think a lot but to love a great deal" (*Life*, ch. 8). And St. Francis de Sales: "Prayer is just knowing how to talk to God, wanting to love Him as best we can; considerations, thinking about Him, is no more than just a way of making you love Him more and as a friend" (*Introduction*, Part 5, ch. 2).

This was the language of common sense in the face of complex speculations, effective and carrying conviction because both these saintly "doctors" had first of all lived what they were teaching; and each of them had formulated living experience in a characteristically structured individual book: the *Introduction to the Devout Life* goes very well, in its way, with St. Teresa's *Life* and *Way of Perfection*. It cannot be said that St. Teresa actually "influenced" St. Francis, but she did most helpfully confirm him in his own approach. What was of the greatest importance for him during those early years was that her wonderful analysis of a soul growing in the mystical life—even though differently— served as a model and guide for Francis' own task of directing ardent and generous souls in their spiritual life. Also, there were her own great gifts as a director more specifically of women; her intuitive insight into the psychology of the prayerful female personality was invaluable to this young director, himself not much older and more experienced than the people he was guiding along new paths. Ultimately they were, of course, doing the same work: helping souls to give greater glory to God in an ever growing and ever more simple love.

For the next six years after the Dijon Lent, and until such time as it seemed right for Madame de Chantal to enter religion, Francis de Sales was thinking out and planning his own new foundation in Savoy. There was a time when it seemed that this might actually be a Carmel but in the end he was left free to use the house that had been donated, the "Galerie" with a garden going down to the Lake of Annecy, for his own Visitation. The rule for the new institute was very much his own, not modeled on that of Carmel, though there were similarities. Though both were contemplative there was to be less penitential hardship so as to allow less robust or older women to enter. There was less emphasis on liturgy—the Little Office, shorter and simpler in its chant—and after the novitiate, a small amount of visiting the poor and the sick. In Savoy the bishop could do as he liked, but the first foundation in France, at nearby Lyons, brought about the change from an informally constituted, simple "institute" to an enclosed order, as was Carmel. The first Carmel in Lyons, however, dates from 1616, a year after the Visitation came there. Enclosure was the condition laid down by the local bishop.

Much has been made to slant the story of this changeover, as though Francis and Madame de Chantal had been forced against their real will to replace an "active" order with a contemplative one: this was not so. The visiting in Annecy which was strictly limited so that each sister was allowed only one month in the year for taking her turn at this duty, was considered right because of local needs and conditions. It was also to be in keeping with the good works to which the women who entered were accustomed in their life in the world: the institute had always been contemplative, but after the Lyons foundation it became even more clearly so. But temperamentally, and as compared with the spirit of the new Spanish Carmels, Francis de Sales had always favored something rather more like compromise: he was no extremist. The argument in Lyons with Archbishop Marquemont—who, it may be noted, had himself been on the point of entering a reformed Carmelite friary in Rome when his appointment as Archbishop of Lyons was announced—was not about "contemplative" or "not contemplative," but about a formal "order" or an informal "institute" without solemn vows. As far as Francis was concerned, small, humble and hidden was beautiful in this respect. But the rapid spread and the large number of Visitation monasteries called for in France, and soon in Italy, Spain and Poland, would in any case have made the informality of the original plan impossible, at any rate in the historical situation of that age of protocol and ceremony. Facile judgments from the vantage-point of our own age are too easy: Mother Teresa of Calcutta, and Charles de Foucauld earlier in the twentieth century, were founders in a completely different social context.

In the spirit of their founders, however, both the Visitation and Carmel successfully resisted the idea of centralized government by a Mother General, and also government by any kindred order of men, an important difference always insisted upon by Teresa of Ávila, Francis de Sales and Madame de Chantal. Carmelites and Visitandines are subject to their local bishop in a not too stringent way, and are happy to accept help or not, as the case may be, from priests of any order or none, that is, local seculars. Help and counsel from a congregation of priests having close spiritual and ideological links with the founders, both of Carmel and of the Visitation, is of course of the greatest possible help, as is especially clear, at any rate for the Visitation, from the situation in the U.S.A., in South America and also in Continental Europe; support and help, however, are not government, a distinction important to the founders concerned. Each Visitation, as, I believe, each Carmel, is accountable to itself alone, not to a group, though they of course keep in helpful touch. Historically speaking, relations between Carmelites and Visitandines have always been creative and good, and, certainly in France and in Spain, both are great readers of their respective founders. French Visitandines will tell you, I think rightly, that the "Little Way" of St. Thérèse of Lisieux—the whole Martin family were great readers of St. Francis de Sales and one of the daughters was a Visitandine—was his characteristic spirituality translated into her own particular nineteenth-century idiom and vocabulary.

The analogies that exist between St. Teresa's *Interior Castle* and St. Francis' *Treatise on the Love of God* would form the subject of another talk. I will just say that St. Francis often refers to St. Teresa whose beatification took place in 1614, two years before the *Treatise* was published, and she was canonized shortly before he died in 1622. He used some of her terms in his book, especially in Books 6 and 7, and though he is profoundly original in his analysis of mystical prayer, he has recourse to her again and again, in the central part, Books 5 to 9, on the prayer of quiet. A special feature of resemblance is their habitual easy cross-reference, if one can call it that, to both the ascetical and the mystical realm as forming one great whole, without watertight compartments, realistically reflecting the actual nature of a growing love of God as they had both lived it and seen it lived in the souls entrusted to their care.

And perhaps most important of all, these two "teacher," that is, "doctor" saints both had to an eminent degree in their different spheres, in all they did and wrote, what can be called "the mind of the Church." This was in the forefront of all their instruction, their analysis and their direction. They were not only two of the greatest mystics but two of the greatest doctors of the Counter-Reformation age, when, as St. Teresa cries out in the preface to the *Way of Perfection*, "the world is on fire!" and she has in mind, as she insists, the harm and havoc the rebel reformers were wreaking and which she wants to counter by helping to give God souls of sacrifice and prayer. She was not, as was St. Francis, a learned theologian but her continual intelligent discourse with learned confessors—both she and St. Francis were carefully selective in the matter of directors for their nuns—over many years had made her very well informed. She was a person who kept on asking questions, and usually the right questions, so as to discover without fear of illusion "the mind of the Church." At the same time, however, both saints had a balanced and robust independence, perhaps they both had the detachment that comes of a most attractive sense of fun, of humor, a capacity to look on the bright side of things. Both were invigorating, full of courage, hope and trust whatever was going on all around them. St. Teresa might well have formulated what is perhaps one of St. Francis de Sales' most famous sayings: "Un saint triste est un triste saint," 'A sad saint is a sorry saint'; but the translation isn't nearly as neat and clever as the original, where a mere change in the position of the adjective transforms meaning. More translatably, St. Teresa just said: "I don't like frowning saints."

NOTES

1. For a detailed analysis, see Pierre Sérouet, O.C.D., *De la vie dévote à la vie mystique: Sainte Thérèse d'Avila, Saint François de Sales*, Études Carmélitaines (Paris, 1958), and F. Charmot, S.J., *Deux maîtres, une spiritualité: Ignace de Loyola, François de Sales* (Paris, 1963). See also *Historia de una santa: Madame de Chantal* (Madrid/Mexico City/Buenos Aires/Pamplona, 1966), the Spanish translation of Elisabeth Stopp, *Madame de Chantal: Portrait of a Saint* (London, 1962/Westminster, Maryland, 1963).

IX

Cor ad cor loquitur:
Newman and St. Francis de Sales

On my way here I met a friend who asked me where I was off to. When I said: "To Birmingham, to give a talk on Newman," his reaction was: "Surely, this is coals to Newcastle?," and of course he was right. I can only hope that the second name in my title provides some sort of excuse for my presence here tonight. And also the fact that these two people, Newman and St. Francis de Sales, widely different though they are in time, place and nationally, have always had this in common for me, and I think for many others who know them at all well: they have always come across to me as real people, known and loved. And this is not only because of their great spiritual and intellectual gifts, their holiness, their pastoral distinction, but quite simply because of their God-given power to conjure themselves up as real, live people in all their writings, above all in their letters, more than 20,000 in Newman's case, and in eleven large volumes of the great Annecy edition of 26 volumes of St. Francis de Sales' works, whose editor, by the way, was an English Benedictine, Dom Benedict Mackey.

It was, then, as friends that both Newman and St. Francis first came across to me, as writers and artists, to use Newman's formulations; "as people creatively thinking out into language . . . what all feel, but all cannot say . . . and this makes them ministers of great benefit to others . . . within the sphere of their personal influence" (*The Idea of a University*, "Literature as the expression of ideas"). Their letters, their treatises, in Newman's case, his written and published sermons, were, and are, "literature," even in translation, always beautifully ordered structures. By their well concealed art—"aim at things," said Newman, "and your words will be right without aiming"—you, the reader, feel and know that you are all the time being personally addressed, involved, caught up and integrated into the process of communication between persons which is what "literature," writing, is about. And in the case of both Newman and St. Francis, this "literature" was essentially pastoral, for souls, for individuals; according to Newman, writing of this kind is always "of a personal character." "A great author," says Newman, "is not just someone who has splendid phrases and is a dealer in words; he is one who has his great or rich visions before him, has something to say and knows how to say it—this is his characteristic and personal gift . . . yet all the time he has with him the charm of simplicity, an incommunicable plainness" that has something mysterious about it. He sees too clearly, however, to be vague; all that he writes is also luminous, clear, consistent. Both these essentially pastoral writers, then, lived so intensely in the spirit, and so constantly realized the presence of the unseen world to which they themselves were hurrying and were guiding other souls, that the words describing their "great and rich visions" came right, and the things they were aiming at were made plain.

Even apart from this major likeness, St. Francis and Newman had other more particular affinities. Both were men of balance, moderation, common sense, though both had a hard battle against an inclination to anger and extreme sensitiveness. Both had a basically joyful view of human nature, they were optimists, both having enjoyed the best kind of humanist education their century could provide, St. Francis at the late Renaissance-oriented universities of Paris and of Padua (St. Francis was born in 1567), Newman at Oxford, both men of brilliant intelligence, in love with classical authors and classical learning, above all, too, with the Church Fathers. Both were what Newman calls "highly educated" in many and diversified fields: St. Francis a lawyer and qualified barrister—he took a double doctorate in law and in theology at Padua where he also used to go to lectures in the famous anatomy theater, the first in Europe and a structure still now standing. He was interested in science, especially in botany

(Padua had a great herb and physic botanical garden) and also in animal life which he observed closely: all those images from God's creation are more than a merely literary convention. The same may apply to Newman's imagery and his metaphorical descriptions: his scientifically informed, terribly accurate analysis of the locust plague in Africa (in his novel, *Callista* [1855]), is one of the great metaphors of evil and sin, one which is close to the atmosphere of the lowest circles in Dante's *Inferno*.

And yet, together with their brilliant, even sophisticated intelligence and psychological expertise, there was in both these writers a true warmth of feeling and sensitivity—this last has been greatly exaggerated for St. Francis (e.g., the *ad nauseam* repeated dictum of his that you catch more flies with a spoonful of honey than a barrel of vinegar) and, I think, wrongly: neither St. Francis nor Newman was in the least sentimental, though both have been sentimentalized (in Newman's case there is the Victorian interpretation and appeal of "Lead, kindly light" and some of the more indifferent poetry—impossible, thank goodness, to sentimentalize the stern rigor of *The Dream of Gerontius*). Both men, too, were mystics who are sometimes denied this title, probably because theirs was very largely the mysticism of the Fathers, straight out of St. John and St. Paul and therefore primarily incarnational, centered on Christ, Our Lord, on His life, His Passion, the Gospels. For St. Francis this incarnational mysticism also stems in a direct line from the late medieval and scholastic tradition; this comes out strongly in the whole of the *Treatise on the Love of God* (1616), especially the opening books. But neither in St. Francis nor in Newman are there any mystical frills, so to speak, or any overweighing via non-scriptural influences. It is true that St. Francis de Sales' greatest disciple and friend, the Cistercian scholar who was also his first and best biographer (Dom Jean de Saint François) was the first to translate Dionysius the Areopagite from Greek into excellent, classical French, with de Sales' encouragement).

Personalities, writers, artists, then, of the stature of Newman and St. Francis de Sales, come across as speaking directly to their readers. The Oratorian Edward Sillem says: "Only he who understands the Cardinal's *cor ad cor loquitur*—the motto comes from a Latin translation of St. Francis' letter on preaching, written to Madame de Chantal's brother, Archbishop André Frémyot, 5 October 1604. Translated into Latin and published as a separate pamphlet, this letter had a wide European circulation, and Newman had quoted from it in his 1855 Dublin Lecture on "University Preaching." In connection with this, Newman quotes, again following St. Francis, from St. Augustine: "The sound of words reaches the ear; the teacher is within, that is, in the heart to which another heart has spoken personally and individually, instructing and moving it." Back to Fr. Sillem: "Only he who understands the Cardinal's *cor ad cor loquitur* and who is prepared to read as though Newman were present in the room actually speaking what you are here and now reading, can come to share Newman's vision of reality with him." Precisely the same applies to St. Francis de Sales. Reading both these writers is a case of coming to experience their "Personal Influence, the Means of Propagating Truth"—this is the significant title of an Oxford University sermon of Newman's, preached at St. Mary's in 1832.

There has never, of course, been any doubt about Newman's greatness as an artist and writer, though there again, it's good to discover that in the new Novena Prayer for his beatification that we have all been saying from 1-9 October this year, his entitlement as a writer comes first in the list of the various capacities in which he "labored to build up God's kingdom"—"as writer, preacher, counselor and educator, Pastor, Oratorian and servant of the poor." Not that Newman would have agreed that the gift of being a writer was necessarily an aid to holiness—rather the contrary: "Saints are not literary men," he wrote to Miss Munro in 1850, firmly disclaiming some other pious lady's attribution to him of sanctity. "Saints are not literary men, they do not love the classics, they do not write Tales. I may be well enough in my way . . . educated, have a peculiar cast of intellect . . . I may have a high view of many things . . . but it is not a high line . . . it is enough for me to black the saints' shoes—if St. Philip uses blacking in heaven." Newman might well here have added the name of St. Francis de Sales as an object of his services as a boot-boy, St. Francis, the man he called "this great and beautiful saint"—Newman was economical in his use of that last adjective; he quite simply loved and revered this saint of his own St. Philip's Counter-Reformation epoch, who, in 1622, just lived to see

St. Philip's canonization. Literary gifts may, of course, quite possibly be a hindrance to becoming a saint; that's not at all improbable. But the writer saint's holiness as revealed in his work, though not conscious, let alone deliberately manifest, is compelling: "The attraction exerted by unconscious holiness," says Newman, "is of an urgent and irresistible nature." Both he and St. Francis de Sales exert that kind of attraction. The Calvinists in the Chablais, the Lake of Geneva region where St. Francis worked so successfully as a young missionary, said that he had "une langue enchanteresse," that what he said and what he wrote in a secretly printed and distributed newsletter week by week cast a spell on reader and listener alike. It still does, just as with Newman: both were masters of the magically memorable phrase, of lucid argument which carries conviction.

It was to this same Chablais region that St. Francis, as Bishop of Geneva, later on invited a group of Oratorian priests whose pastoral and educational work he knew personally through Bérulle and the Paris Oratory. The bishop's plan did not come off but he founded, instead, his *Sainte Maison,* a "hallowed house," at Thonon, an educational, religious center for lay people organized by secular priests. This had marked Oratorian traits. St. Francis certainly had a strong sense of kinship with St. Philip's aims in their common work of spiritual renewal among lay people, as a direct result of which both of them founded a congregation or society for which neither of them wanted the label of an "order." When it first started in Annecy in 1610 with Madame de Chantal, her two friends and a lay sister from Geneva, St. Francis de Sales' Visitation had a clear lay orientation built into its contemplative structure. But the historical situation of Catholicism in Counter-Reformation France and in Newman's Victorian England is too diverse for me to make any useful comparison—in a few brief words—of all that they both achieved for lay people and for actually helping to transform their role and sense of identity within the structure of the Church. The one important thing is that both St. Francis and Newman, each in their own original and quietly revolutionary way, aimed at the edification of the ordinary, everyday laity of their time, encouraging them (again quoting the title of one of Newman's sermons) in "Doing Glory to God in Pursuit of the World," and doing this in the most committed way possible. St. Francis' attempt to "introduce" lay people systematically to the devout life, writing a book specially for them, to show people in family life, in workshops, in the professions, the way to true spirituality, to a prayerful love of God—this was frowned upon in many quarters as an exaggeration, something outlandish and new, at any rate to begin with. It must be taken into account that St. Francis was really a kind of foreigner in France and for the French hierarchy: he was a Savoyard, and as bishop, he was subject to an Italian duke and ecclesiastic in Milan, a fact often forgotten. I need not remind you that Newman in his attempts to "educate, widen and refine" the minds of English Catholics got into some trouble when he proposed the idea of "Consulting the Faithful in Matters of Doctrine" (the title of his essay in the July number of *The Rambler* in 1859). If the laity is to be consulted, it must be helped to greater spiritual awareness well beyond what was considered its rightful province: "to hunt, shoot and entertain" (Msgr. Talbot's letter to Manning in 1866).[1]

Newman's choice of a motto from this like-minded Counter-Reformation admirer of his own founder, St. Philip, rested on a general kinship of attitude, not on a close knowledge of actual texts. He owned copies of both the *Introduction to a Devout Life* and *Treatise on the Love of God*, in English translation but he does not seem to have known St. Francis' books really well. But *cor ad cor loquitur* is an insight of wider significance. It is not only about the priest-teacher's, the pastor's heart speaking directly to the hearts of those in his charge before God, be they listeners or readers; it involves the writer's own heart speaking to God, and God's to him. "You see, Theotimus," says St. Francis to the God-fearing soul whom he addresses by name throughout his *Treatise* (interesting that the introductory book is addressed to Philothea, emphasizing the soul's *love*, while in the mystical book the soul has got as far as the seeming paradox of the loving *fear* of God), "mystical theology is about speaking and listening to God in the silence of the heart; and because this is a matter of very secret aspirations and inspirations, it is called a dialogue of silence; eyes speak to eyes, heart to another heart, and no one hears what is said in this silent language except the lovers themselves" (*Treatise*, Bk. 6, ch. 1). The extent to which both St. Francis de

Sales and Newman exemplified this personal, heart-to-heart dialogue attitude to God, the Creator, needs no further comment. Both were men of prayer but were also actively involved in a lifelong career of instruction, of teaching minds and hearts, and St. Francis was in 1877, within Newman's lifetime, declared a Doctor of the Church. Both men were dedicated teachers, pedagogues in the best sense of that term, teachers of spirituality and skilled in the use of words that aim, as Newman puts it "at imprinting on the heart what will never leave it," in contrast to "mere sentiment which can transfer an emotion from mind to mind but is not able to fix it there" (Dublin Discourse). In her *Testimony* (1629, edited in English translation 1967) St. Jane Frances de Chantal said of her director: "He used such precise and easily understood terms in speaking about God that he made people grasp very readily the most delicate and subtle truths of the spiritual life. . . . His words moved both heart and will, he made people live by the truths he explained in such clear, heartfelt terms." St. Francis also spoke very clearly to Newman, one might say, was close to him within the words of his chosen motto, embroidered on his Cardinal's scarlet vestment, at the ceremonies in Rome in the spring of 1879. He was there as a friendly presence at a great moment, and thereafter, too, in his chapel at home in Birmingham and right to the end in the *cor ad cor loquitur* on the funeral pall at Rednal in August 1890, when images gave way to truth.

In the private chapel partitioned off in Newman's room here in the Birmingham Oratory, there is a portrait of St. Francis de Sales in the important central position behind the altar. Based on the Turin portrait of 1618 it can be called a personal interpretation of the saint rather more than a mere copy, the work of an artist who had clearly studied other portraits of St. Francis de Sales and also his personality as it comes across in the accounts of his life and in his writings. This interesting portrait is the work of Miss Maria Rosina Giberne, a family friend of the Newmans who later in life entered the Visitation at Autun in Burgundy, close to the castle of Monthelon where Madame de Chantal lived in her early widowhood and where the memory of both the founder saints always was, and still now is very much alive. Over the mantelpiece in Newman's study there is a photograph of

Miss Giverne as Sister Maria Pia in her Visitation habit; it is one of a large number of photographs of Newman's friends pinned to the walls in what might be called a fearless clutter. On the wall to the left of the door, in a position where Newman had a good view of them as he sat at his desk in the center of the room, there are a whole number of sepia-tinted lithographs. They depict well-known scenes from the life of St. Francis de Sales, and again it is an interesting and personal point of view that is presented here in the genre of French nineteenth-century historical drawing, remote from pre-Raphaelite romanticism but tending rather more towards the classical, humanist tradition and therefore to a truer view of the saint. The artist was again Maria Giberne and it was through her artistic skill and insight that Newman's mind could dwell habitually on the example of sanctity in the life of St. Francis de Sales.

Newman had some contact with the English Visitation, then in the West country, now in Sussex, through Sister Mary Dominica Bowden, the daughter of his friends, John and Elizabeth. He corresponded with her and he used regularly to offer his Mass for the Visitation on the feast day of both St. Francis de Sales and St. Jane Frances de Chantal. Newman's memory is very much alive, too, in the monastery of the Visitation in Wilmington, Delaware. This was the first contemplative, that is, non-teaching house of the order to be founded in the States. The foundation took place in 1892 under the aegis of the remarkable second Bishop of Wilmington, Alfred Allen Curtis, who was greatly devoted to Newman. As an Episcopalian minister in Baltimore he had read and been powerfully influenced by Newman's writings and his personality. In 1871 he resigned his office and early in the following year he made the long journey to England so as to meet Newman and talk things over with him, knowing that in his Anglican days, he had written a long essay on "The Anglo-American Church," published in "The British Critic" of 1839. After a visit to Oxford and Littlemore, Curtis stayed at the Birmingham Oratory for some time and was received into the Church by Newman himself, then confirmed by Bishop Ullathorne. Two years later when Curtis was ordained after study at the Sulpician Seminary in Baltimore, he was able to produce as evidence of his reception and conditional baptism the certificate which Newman had written out for him in his own hand. Through Bishop Curtis' spirituality and his preaching and teaching, Newman, as a "person," is present now at Wilmington in ways hearteningly noticeable to someone who loves both Newman and the founders of the Visitation. At his own wish the bishop was buried in the cemetery within the enclosure of the Visitation.[2]

In conclusion I would like to say a word or two about St. Francis de Sales' role as a bridge and mediator between Catholics and Anglicans, a role of which Newman was aware. In the words of Henry Dodwell, an Anglican divine and professor at Oxford who translated the *Introduction to the Devout Life* (albeit "fitted for the use of Protestants") in 1673, "It is more in the interest of healing differences to contrive devotional books which may be serviceable to all good Christians which otherwise would only advance a single party" (preface to his translation of the *Introduction*). Feeling that he had always been "a son of the Church," Newman agreed to the republication of his Anglican sermons with that same idea of "healing differences" and in the same spirit. In Victorian and Edwardian times St. Francis de Sales was thought of as an uncontroversial figure, a spiritual teacher who was an acceptable, indeed attractive Papist, in whose spirituality all could meet. His best and most readable translators in those days were Anglicans, and the first Anglican Sisterhood, Dr. Neale's Society of St. Margaret, founded in 1854, based its Rule on that of St. Francis de Sales for the Visitation before it became a cloistered order. He had the appeal of a man who could write attractively and with calm authority not only about prayer and the devout life, but about the ethics of married life, about social relations and community living, even on conservation; at home in a landscape of forest, lakes and mountains, he had a Franciscan openness to nature and to the beauty of God's created world. He was one of the great—and the few—secular priest saints of his time, accessible to all, of universal Christian appeal. In his own personal way, one may say that Newman too responded warmly to the appeal of this "great and beautiful saint."

NOTES

1. See the articles in the May 1987 number of *The Friends of Cardinal Newman Newsletter*, as well as Fr. Charles Stephen Dessain's pamphlet *Cardinal Newman, the Oratory and the Laity*.

2. In 1993 the Wilmington Visitation relocated to Tyringham, Massachusetts. At that time Bishop Curtis' remains were transferred to the Cathedral Cemetery in Wilmington.

X

THE CONTEXT OF ECUMENISM

After the Second Vatican Council St. Francis de Sales' feast day was moved from 29th January to the 24th with the result that he is now commemorated during the Week of Prayer for Christian Unity. In view of his deep and passionate commitment to the cause of recovering unity among all Christians, there is surely a connection to be made. It can be made by considering St. Francis' attitude and linking it with the Council's *Decree on Ecumenism* (1964) in the hope that this may more clearly point the way to the basic pattern for the return of unity among Christians, that of the Three in One and of Christ's prayer that all might be one as He Himself is one with the Father and the Holy Spirit.

Just before Christmas 1608 (18 or 19 December) St. Francis wrote a letter to Madame de Chantal, then still living in Burgundy with her children. The bearer of this letter was his younger brother, Bernard de Sales, who was about to sign his marriage contract with the baroness' daughter, Marie-Aimée de Chantal. The translator of the *Selected Letters* (1960) did think about including this letter in her selection but decided that it was perhaps not quite in keeping with the ecumenical spirit of the time even in pre-Council days. However, the fact remains that this letter was considered sufficiently important to be sent to Rome and form a part of the cause for the first canonization process of 1628, a cause still supervised by Madame de Chantal herself and her advisers in Annecy. Saying something about this letter goes to the heart of the problem of "ecumenism" in late Counter-Reformation

times of religious strife and warfare at the beginning of the
seventeenth century in France.

In the opening paragraph of this letter St. Francis writes
about the happiness of Bernard de Sales at the prospect of a truly
Catholic marriage on which every blessing is called down, and
then goes on to point to a sad contrast:

> But what a hard transition it is for my spirit to pass from
> this marriage to the dissolution of poor Madame Bareul's
> marriage with her God! So this poor little lady and her
> husband want to go to perdition! The *Confessions* of
> St. Augustine, and especially the chapter I pointed out to
> her when I saw her, would have been enough to restrain
> her, had the reasons she alleges really been her only
> motive for throwing herself into this abyss. On the day of
> His great judgment God will show her His justice and will
> surely make quite clear His reasons for abandoning her.
> Ah! Deep calls unto deep! (Ps 42:8) I shall pray to God
> for her, especially on the feast day of St. Thomas, begging
> him, by his happy unbelief to intercede for this poor soul
> who is so unhappily an unbeliever (*Oeuvres*, 14:93-94).

The "poor little lady" in question was Madame de Chantal's
cousin. He had met her earlier that same year when her difficulties
about the faith were already a cause of concern and were discussed
with her cousin's director. In his letter he goes on to say how
thankful he himself ought to be that exposed as he was to reading
"all those pestiferous books at a vulnerable and volatile age when
his mind was young and frail," he had remained quite unmoved
by this "miserable malady of doubt," which, by the way, could
not be said of his correspondent who suffered a lifelong torture
of doubts against the faith. But he tries to hearten and comfort her:

> Let us calm down and be at peace, dear Daughter, about
> the loss of those souls; Our Lord Jesus Christ, to whom
> they were dearer still, would not have allowed them to
> go their own way had it not all been for His own greater
> glory in some way. But we must certainly mourn their
> loss and sigh for them as David for his Absalom, hanged

and lost . . . . but there are times when we simply can't keep a really firm hold on ourselves in the face of events so deserving of horror (*Oeuvres*, 14:94).

His pastoral concern makes him add that the poor little lady ought nevertheless still to be urged to read the letters of St. Jerome, for quite apart from the power of specific arguments, the spirit of the Fathers always breathes against the very atmosphere of heresy:

> The other day, very early in the morning, a most learned man came to see me and tell me how God had delivered him from heresy: "I had," so he told me, "the most learned bishop in the world as my catechist." So I was expecting him to name one of the great reputations of our time, but lo and behold, the name he came out with was that of St. Augustine (*Oeuvres*, 14:94-95).

Her director tells Madame de Chantal this story so as to make clear to her that the Fathers quite simply have an anti-heretical aura about them. He also makes the point that "whoever preaches with love preaches adequately against heretics, even if he doesn't bring out a single word of argument directed against them. . . all that the Fathers wrote is good and proper for the conversion of heretics" (*Oeuvres*, 14:96-97).

I have talked about this letter of 1608 at some length because it sets the scene for any historical, positive and fruitful thinking about St. Francis de Sales in the context of ecumenism. There is no bypassing the fact that for him, those who had left the one true faith and Church were heretics, that is, people who had willfully "chosen for themselves" (the root word being the Greek "to choose"), and opted out in a spirit of rebellion and pride from the "Catholic" Church, that is, the Church for all, universally embracing all, *kathalon*, "for all." This was an abhorrent and terrible tragedy, like Absalom's end, but allowed by God for His ultimate greater glory in some way hidden from us, and mysterious. At the same time the letter shows the only possible, though seemingly less direct way of approach to the tragedy: that of prayer and love.

In his sermon on the occasion of his installation as provost of the Geneva cathedral chapter in December 1593, Francis said: "The walls of Geneva must be broken down by charity and it is by charity that we must invade this city and recover it . . . Let our camp not be one of war but let it be God's camp where the trumpets ring out loud and clear: Holy, holy, holy is the Lord of Hosts. . . It is by our own hunger and thirst, not by that of a beleaguered enemy that we must repel our adversaries. It is by prayer that we shall drive him out, for that kind of demon only yields to prayer and fasting" (*Oeuvres*, 7:107-108). But even though prayer, penance and lifelong sacrifice were his main weapons, he remained "the hammer of heretics," a man who saw the change of religion as something wholly negative, was opposed to anything remotely resembling religious liberty or even mere social and civic tolerance. It was his firmly held opinion that no Catholic prince should tolerate any religion other than his own in his lands: Protestants should be, and in fact were, deprived of public office and even exiled from their own homeland if they were unresponsive to what St. Francis rather nicely called "une douce violence" to persuade them to return to the one true fold. In the meanwhile he supported his loving prayer and penance by very hard work in his preaching and writing, structuring ideas, arguments in his persuasively organized writings and sermons to enlighten, explain and to carry conviction where he saw a tragic need for a change of heart and mind.

Even though St. Francis' basic requirements of prayer and sacrifice have not changed, the emphasis has shifted away from the negative concepts of "heresy" and "conversion" to the idea of unity and therefore of a new kind of reunion between all those who are followers of Jesus Christ. The model is far more clearly that of a pilgrim Church moving steadily towards Christ, with an admission of guilt and sin on both sides for the healing of which a change of heart is essential. This is movement forward along ways which are still not clear to us, rather than a movement of return to former entrenched positions, the only possible solution to be envisaged after the Council of Trent and in the lifetime of a Catholic bishop of St. Francis de Sales' times. The idea of a Vatican Council publishing a *Decree on Ecumenism*, a word which he would in any case have understood only in its original connotation as describing the general councils of the early Church in the time of the Fathers, would have been a matter of astonishment and even bewilderment to him. Had he read and studied the 1964 decree, however, he would soon have found himself in calmer waters, more especially when he got to the central section, "Ecumenism in practice," following on the introductory statement of "Catholic principles of Ecumenism" and followed by the concluding chapter, "Churches and ecclesial communities separated from the Apostolic See of Rome." I quote some of the sentences (from the CTS translation [London, 1965]) which would have seemed particularly familiar and relevant to a man of St. Francis de Sales' mind:

> Every renewal in the Church consists essentially in an increase of loyalty to its vocation . . . in continual reformation . . . this is the reason for the movement towards unity (n. 6).

> The value of the efforts towards unity of all Christ's faithful is in proportion to the purity of their own personal desire to order their own lives on the Gospel (n. 7).

> The method and manner of presenting Catholic belief (important in the formation of priests, in the teaching of sacred theology) should be such as to prove no obstacle to dialogue with the brethren. What is absolutely necessary is that the whole teaching be expressed with lucidity . . . it should be presented with greater depth and accuracy, in such language which allows separated brethren to obtain a true grasp of it (n. 11).

> All Catholics must make Christian perfection their aim and, each in his own degree, strive for the daily cleansing and renewal of the Church which carries the lowly and dying state of Jesus in its body until Christ shall summon it into His presence in all its beauty, no stain, no wrinkle, to use St. Paul's words . . . In all things we must cultivate charity" (n. 4).

Sentences of this kind really do amount to something like a checklist of the ways in which Francis de Sales, as Pope Paul VI said in 1967, can rightly be described as "a precursor of Vatican II,"[1] though at the same time it is clear that such descriptions of him lose all validity unless the precise historical moment of his life and of his ecclesiastical career are kept in mind. There is also the fact that we too, in making judgments and pronouncements of this kind, are caught up in the historical process of our own day and age. The Decree issues a warning that there must be "no false attitudes of appeasement": St. Francis de Sales would not be expected, now, any more than in his own time, to compromise on any point of doctrine, or on the basic truth which we assert, indeed must assert, that the one "ecumenical" Church is, and always has been since its foundation by Jesus Christ, present, here and now. The present use of the word "ecumenical" as "belonging to or representing the whole Christian world," and therefore envisaging the "reunion" and ultimate "unity" of all Christians, only dates from the early part of the twentieth century. It now stands for all that we *can* and *do* share with all Christians, rather than for what divides us; it stands for Christian fellowship, for our sharing in good works, in study groups, especially of our now shared Bible translation, in conferences and publications, and in specially intensive get-together exercises, such as the January Week of Prayer for Christian Unity. Far are the days when her director had to advise Madame de Chantal on the propriety, or otherwise, of accepting an invitation to dinner with a heretic, and exactly how measured to make the friendliness in conversation when they met.

Now back to the checklist of directives from the *Decree on Ecumenism* and how they relate to St. Francis de Sales. Firstly, the reformation of the Catholic Church. Quite naturally, as a young missionary and later on throughout his career as a bishop and prince of a Catholic see in exile from his own territory, he had to observe discretion in this matter in his *written* word; his lifelong *action*, however, speaks for itself. His model in this and his inspiration was St. Charles Borromeo to whom he was deeply devoted (the only medal he ever had on his rosary, and it was there at the time of his death, was one of St. Charles). St. Francis worked untiringly for the better training of his priests, he reformed religious orders, he himself founded one on an entirely new model, he was assiduous in visiting, often at great personal peril, even the most remote and mountainous parishes in his Alpine diocese, he radically reformed his own episcopal household, his episcopal "palace" being a small rented house which he ran on almost Franciscan lines of holy poverty and hidden simplicity; he fulfilled his primary episcopal duty—that of teaching, instruction and example—with untiring zeal, both in the spoken and the written word. In his Chablais flysheets (1595-96), printed on a secret press and distributed at night from door to door, he made what was probably, it seems, the first attempt at a real dialogue with the Calvinists. Known as *Les Controverses* when first rediscovered and used as evidence in his first canonization process, but now republished under the more irenical and ecumenical title of *Méditations sur l'Église* or *Mémorial sur l'Église* (1958), titles used by him in letters mentioning the flysheets, they constitute a clear, firm and beautifully written analysis of the doctrinal teaching of the Church.[2] Information is structured in question and answer form, supported by concise logical argument, sometimes reinforced by extremely funny but unhurtful satire but there was never any crude verbal abuse or hostility—a desideratum now taken for granted in "ecumenical" argument but a unique effort in its own time—proving, in the words of the 1964 Decree, "no obstacle to dialogue with the brethren . . . expressed with lucidity and with greater depth and linguistic accuracy."

As to the Decree directives that the ecumenist is to model his life on the Gospel, to imitate his Lord Jesus Christ as best he can, to cultivate charity in all things—here the saint's whole life and work bear witness: St. Francis de Sales himself was intensely aware that the love and sacrifice of a Christocentric life was the essential basis for any fruitful apostolate. And this brings me to the final point to be made: what are the reasons, apart from this overriding and overall one of his sanctity and his love, that have made this saint of Counter-Reformation times a figure of such great ecumenical appeal, "a man to heal the differences" in the words of Henry Dodwell, the Anglican professor at Oxford who in 1673 translated the *Introduction to a Devout Life*, "fitted for the use of Protestants."[3] St. Francis was an outstanding writer and artist in words, the author of an all-time spiritual best-seller for the laity which has reached far beyond his own Catholic Church and "the controversies embroiling the schools . . . contriving devotional books which may be serviceable to all good Christians which otherwise would advance a single party," as Dodwell puts it.

Another translator in the Protestant camp, William Nicholls, gives a clue (1701) to a further reason why the *Introduction* had this strong ecumenical appeal. St. Francis was and still is, as far as the general reader of spiritual books is concerned, a man of one book, and the fact that he also wrote an outstanding work of mystical theology, the *Treatise on the Love of God*, tends to be forgotten, as is also the fact that his first book, in a hidden way, so clearly points to what was yet to come, and that the same can be said of his great correspondence. But William Nicholls can deal with this difficulty: "This Popish Bishop is one of their best writers and does not run into the mystical stuff of Teresa, Blosius, Sancta Sophia etc., though Sales has a little of it too, which I have left out." One might make the comment here that the ecumenist of our time is, in fact, very interested in "the mystical stuff" of, for instance, St. John of the Cross, St. Teresa and also St. Francis de Sales himself: he tends to see this as common ground and territory of all Christians, indeed, of non-Christians, too.

But St. Francis de Sales, the mystic, and his contemplative Order, too, remain comparatively hidden, and that is, no doubt, as he would have wished things to be. His best-seller, however, was written explicitly for the laity, again, a most important factor in post-Counter-Reformation times. In the popular consciousness he remains the acceptable popish gentleman-saint, one of the great and the few secular saints, that is, a priest not belonging to an Order in his own time, a man accessible to all, of universal, that is, ecumenical appeal. And this appeal was already there as long ago as the reign of King James I in England, and in a century when Protestants and Catholics were still busy hanging and burning one another in the name of the same Lord and Saviour who had prayed that all might be one. This saint's appeal was that of a man in close touch with lay people of every rank, with men and women, with family life, who could write attractively and with calm authority on morals, on marriage, on social relations and community living, even on conservation and life on the land, a man who came from what would now be called "landed gentry," having a Franciscan openness to the whole world of nature. The appeal of such a man was bound to be great and lasting far beyond all man-made barriers of religious creed and allegiance. Humanism comes well before doctrine in matters of ecumenism, a matter not just of the intellect but of the heart, and this is where St. Francis de Sales scored so greatly in his own time of tragically divided religious strife, and still scores now, at a time when differences seem less tragic, less acute, quite simply because Christian belief is no longer, for the generality, at least, a matter of intense commitment and allegiance.

Here, too, St. Francis de Sales' convincing and lovable kind of holiness has much to appeal and therefore also much to teach, as has been the case for centuries now. The Dominican, Père Yves Congar, one day speculated what François de Sales, in his rightful capacity as Ordinary of his own see in Geneva, and thus responsible for the Permanent Personnel of the Ecumenical Council of Churches in that city, would now say if he were invited to address this Council. What kind of sermon would he preach during the Week of Prayer for Christian Unity in January, in the middle of which his feast day now falls? What comment would he make on the Vatican II Decree? "We can be sure of one thing," said Père Yves, "his every thought and word would be dictated by his charity and his sole purpose and desire would be to follow the indications of God's will. Ecumenism claims no other justification."[4]

NOTES

1. Pope Paul VI makes this observation in his apostolic letter *Sabaudiae gemma*, published on the occasion of the fourth centenary of the birth of St. Francis de Sales (1967).

2. See the essay *"Meditations on the Church* (1595-96)," in the present volume.

3. On St. Francis de Sales' Protestant translators, see the essay "Healing Differences: St. Francis de Sales in Seventeenth-Century England" in the present volume.

4. For the complete text, see Yves M.-J. Congar, O.P., "S. François de Sales aujourd'hui," *Choisir* (July-August, 1962): 24-26, and the English translation which was published in *Salesian Studies*, vol. 3, no.1 (Winter 1966): 5-9.